'Today's organizations are more like fighter squadrons than we realize. Nothing goes perfectly for long. Human intervention is required all the time. Yet many organizations try to operate with highly centralized rules in the belief that, when those rules are adjusted correctly, it will run on autopilot with great efficiency and effectiveness.

The team-based approach that gives fighter squadrons their agility, security and performance achieves the same results in our organizations. They out-think, out-plan and out-maneuver the opposition. They have everyone involved to the fullest possible extent. They achieve a competitive advantage because everyone is helping to achieve it.

Early in my military career, I learned the value and necessity of strong leadership and commitment, and the value of using teams to build them. To lead a team is not just to decide the right things to do, but to creating the dynamics in which people commit themselves, energetically and enthusiastically to bring those things about.

Boo and Murph are experts at creating high performing teams and they know how to operate in highly complex and rapidly changing environments. *On Time On Target* gives everyone a repeatable process to create these favourable dynamics and high performing teams. I commend it to you.'

Air Marshal (Ret) Geoff Brown AO,
former Chief of Air Force,
Royal Australian Air Force

'Our PepsiCo leadership team has leveraged Jim Murphy's Afterburner frameworks and lessons learned to enhance our executional excellence; from how we plan to our execution at the point of purchase.'

PepsiCo Americas Foods

'The concepts "Brief, Execute, Debrief" were so relevant to our business that I find our staff now applying these approaches in their daily business dealings.'

AMGen

'Proven tactics and techniques to drive business success by applying military principles, some of which we've deployed at The Home Depot . . . Jim [Murphy] understands that at the heart of every strategy . . . at the core of every successful campaign . . . are people.'

The Home Depot

'You can't travel far in corporate America without hearing about Jim Murphy and the radical things he and his company are doing. Murphy is the hands down voice of successful companies and elite corporate warriors everywhere.'

L. Douglas Keeney, former Vice President,
Young & Rubicam, author of 15 *Minutes*

'It's a paradigm shift . . . To me, any methodology that can drive clarity in the organization with accountability built into it—it's just a big win.'

VMware, Inc.

'On face value, military planning couldn't be further removed from a family owned business working in the wine industry. Yet we have already incorporated some of the key thinking presented in this book around executing an air force "mission", such as re-framing the way we approach debriefs within our teams so that we can capture lessons learned for next time.'

Brown Brothers Wines

'The Afterburner team and their "PLAN–BRIEF–EXECUTE–DEBRIEF" methodology have taken the Pfizer sales approach and promoted new levels of accountability and improvement.'

Pfizer Australia

'At Interlink we like to be the best in the tolling industry. Our business is somewhat like the world fighter pilots: it needs to be agile and fast to keep up with the increasing demands of our modern business world. Our people need to communicate well, coordinate a demanding range of resources, learn and improve on past performance. Afterburner provides a proven approach that I believe can keep us at the leading edge in terms of business practices.'

Rex Wright, General Manager, Interlink Roads

'Flex is a novel approach to engaging the team dynamic that provides plenty of fun, serious takeaway messages, and practical approaches to improving team performance and focus on core mission. Highly recommend it.'

Australia and New Zealand Banking Group

'Flex opened a new perspective to the way health professionals plan, execute and measure outcomes of daily practice.'

International Collaboration for Excellence
in Critical Care Medicine

JAMES D. MURPHY is the author of the bestselling *Flawless Execution*. He is the CEO of Afterburner Inc., the consulting firm he founded after eight years as an F-15 fighter pilot with the U.S. Air Force. Afterburner has appeared in *Inc.* Magazine's 'Inc. 500 List' twice, and was recognized in 2016 by Forbes as a 'Best Small Company in America'.

CHRISTIAN BOUCOUSIS is the CEO of Afterburner Australia. He served as an F/A-18 fighter pilot for eleven years with the Royal Australian Air Force, and now owns property development company Mode Developments with projects in Sydney, Perth and Papua New Guinea.

JAMES D. MURPHY
CHRISTIAN BOUCOUSIS

ON TIME ON TARGET

HOW TEAMS AND COMPANIES CAN CUT THROUGH COMPLEXITY AND GET THINGS DONE ... THE FIGHTER PILOT WAY

ALLEN&UNWIN
SYDNEY • MELBOURNE • AUCKLAND • LONDON

First published in 2016

Allen & Unwin
83 Alexander Street
Crows Nest NSW 2065
Australia
Phone: (61 2) 8425 0100
Email: info@allenandunwin.com
Web: www.allenandunwin.com

Cataloguing-in-Publication details are available
from the National Library of Australia
www.trove.nla.gov.au

ISBN 978 1 76029 384 0

Set in 12/16 pt Fairfield LH 45 Light by Post Pre-press Group, Australia
Printed and bound in Australia by Griffin Press

10 9 8 7 6 5 4 3 2 1

MIX
Paper from
responsible sources
FSC
www.fsc.org
FSC® C009448

The paper in this book is FSC® certified.
FSC® promotes environmentally responsible,
socially beneficial and economically viable
management of the world's forests.

This book is dedicated to the courageous men and women in our armed forces who have represented our countries 'down range'. Your sacrifices secure our right to live freely, and your discipline inspires us.

CONTENTS

AUTHORS' PREFACE

FROM MURPH

As an American fighter pilot, I flew the U.S. Air Force F-15 Eagle—a supersonic jet with twin afterburning engines. Flying the F-15 or any fighter jet is, literally, unlike anything on earth. They are purpose-built to carry 20 tons of plane and ammunition around tight corners at 1200 miles per hour (1932 kilometers per hour). If I scramble to the jet, jump in, crank up the engines, scan the switches and dials in my cockpit, and push up the throttle to full afterburner, I can be in a vertical climb through 15,000 feet in a matter of seconds. Once airborne, I'm flying a jet capable of dogfighting on either side of the sound barrier. I can fly high enough to see the curvature of the earth, or fly 500 feet off the ground in the black of night. Either way, when this jet and I are in groove, I am comfortable, at one with the F-15.

The key word is 'when'—*when* we work together. A supersonic jet is a temperamental beast, built for speed and agility. Those attributes give it advantages, but there's a price. Pilots have razor-thin margins for error, and we're constantly testing them. That demands undivided attention. Yet we're also checking terrain clearance, radar, weapons selection, navigation, tracking the enemy, and managing avionics. So we're sharp, alert; our situational awareness crackling like fireworks. Get anything wrong, and it's game over.

That sounds like we're up there alone, but no. When you're flying a mission, you're flying with your squadron and possibly leading it; all the time flying to a plan and assessing it, responding to threats, making decisions, communicating them, all the time working in sync with a team whose every movement and word is understood. And that mission plan is part of something bigger, something you're willing to die for, something that relies on you doing all you can to execute your mission, flawlessly. That's what we do. The world of a fighter pilot is life at Mach One—fast, often thrilling, but absolutely disciplined and unforgiving. Being able to handle this, mentally and physically, is something that all fighter pilots are proud of.

So what does it take to be a fighter pilot? Not what you'd think from watching *Top Gun*. When I first flew an Eagle I was only 23 years old. I was a college kid with okay grades. Fifteen months before I flew the F-15 I had never touched an airplane. I'm no math genius and I'm probably no better coordinated than you. I stay in shape, though probably no better shape than you. But I went through a process. I followed a process perfected over more than five decades that made me a fighter pilot.

From my first day as a fighter pilot, I have studied that process. I worked using it and taught it for over eight years with the U.S. Air Force (USAF), seeing twenty nations follow the process in the toughest of simulated conditions, the international Flag exercises. I got my first post-air force job with it, broke sales records because of it, and finally set up my own company, Afterburner, following its principles. That was twenty years ago, a milestone all entrepreneurs are proud of, and I've learned a lot more over the years about the power and confidence that this disciplined process, Flex, can offer. The more complex and uncertain the times, the more Flex offers: agile and rock-solid in one.

FROM BOO

It's three in the afternoon and storm clouds are gathering over the airfield. Dark grey and heavy with precipitation, the thunder cells roll in relentlessly towards 'Fighter Town', Royal Australian Air Force (RAAF) Base Williamtown, north of Sydney on the Australian east coast. The afternoon's flying programs have been cancelled and all the squadron's aircraft are on the ground. A glum afternoon for everyone.

Except me. My face is splitting with a huge grin as I fly my jet up vertically beside a towering cumulonimbus, feeling weightless in the cockpit. I'm supposed to be flying a set 'profile' or mission, with clear objectives to test the aircraft's performance. But the weather is awful and there's no clear airspace. So I decide to do something I haven't really done in 30 months of training: just have fun. I engage full afterburner on the 20-tonne fire breathing war chariot, or F/A-18 Hornet as the engineers call it, raw fuel is dumped into the engine exhaust, nearly doubling the jet's power. I am going straight up and I am not slowing down.

This is only my fourth flight in the Hornet and the first time I've been solo. Just 21-year-old me, feeling like Armstrong, Aldrin, and Collins (all fighter pilots) as they launched Apollo 11 for the moon.

I look down over my shoulder, see a gap in the clouds and manage to descend. This is part of my profile: slow the aircraft to 200 knots (370 kilometers per hour), descend to 250 feet (80ish metres), and push the throttle to FULL AB. Full Afterburner. No longer Buzz Aldrin cruising to the moon, now I feel like a pod racer from *Star Wars*. The acceleration is insane. I'm thrown back into the seat and in no time I'm back over 500 knots—over

930 kilometers per hour. I'm pulling 4 G, four times the force of gravity; check forward on the stick and for a moment I am flying at 1000 kilometers per hour—straight up. Giddy up!

Slight problem. I am now 'joker' fuel: I have only enough gas to get back to the airfield or, if the weather is too bad, fly down to RAAF Base Richmond in Sydney's north-west. How much would I be in the poop for diverting to an alternate airfield on my first solo? That isn't in the profile. Not to mention I haven't been qualified to fly in cloud yet . . .

No time for 'what-ifs'. Time to park the nirvana of the last few minutes and focus on what's ahead. What have I learned in those 30 months? What's the situation NOW, make a DECISION, then ACT. I decide I've got to keep sight of the ground. So I pull back on the stick and shoot back down the same hole in the cloud that I'd just punched through vertically.

The weather gods are with me and I manage to 'scud run' under the low cloud, thumping decibels as the exhaust rips the air apart and its sound bounces between the clouds and the ground below. It's a low approach, about half the altitude of what I've landed with an instructor. What is my SITUATION, make a DECISION, ACT. I bring the heavy jet in for a firm landing on the wet runway. BOOM, lightning strikes about 10 metres off the wing tip as I roll out to slow the aircraft and exit the runway.

It's just me as the rain starts dumping down on the big bubble canopy—the 21-year-old average joe from Brisbane, who was pulling beers in a bar before this job, who managed to sneak airborne 30 minutes ago, and was the only bloke in the entire country airborne in a fighter jet at that moment, realizing a lifelong dream.

So what? What I'd learned is that the fear of uncertainty is no match for the air force's disciplined process I'd been taught. I'd proven to myself that unfamiliar territory could be made familiar if you follow that process. I'd been able to make quick decisions—the right decisions—and act on them before my situation changed to make them the wrong ones. And I would never forget it.

I served for eleven years as a pilot in the Royal Australian Air Force, and now this is my eleventh year as an entrepreneur. I look back and recall the hundreds of times in those years that I've felt uncomfortable, let down, a failure, confronted, scared, embarrassed, or at a tough crossroad. Every time I've been able to fall back on a very simple fighter pilot discipline, and managed to get through, wiser for the experience. I hope you enjoy this book, and use it. This stuff works.

PART A

INTRODUCING FLEX

THE ORIGINS OF FLEX

Flex is our label for a way of thinking and a framework for action. Though the term is not used in the military, its DNA stems from the disciplines and mindsets of special military teams: U.S. Navy SEALs, Australian SAS, U.S. Army Rangers and, of course, jet fighter pilots in army, navy, marine, and air force squadrons.

These teams are geared to act as tight, effective units in hostile, complex, and dynamic environments. All of these teams would recognize and use the principles in this book, though they may have their own terms for them. These are the principles that we learned in the U.S. Air Force and the Royal Australian Air Force, and they are common to all of the air forces that fly alongside them: the Royal Air Force of the United Kingdom, the Royal Canadian Air Force, and the fighter pilots of Brazil, Chile, Malaysia, Singapore, Thailand, India, Israel, Italy, Greece, France, the Netherlands, Argentina, and any others involved in joint military exercises and campaigns with the U.S. or Australian air forces. Any fighter pilot on the planet would recognize these principles, and be able to work together using them. They are how fighter pilots think and act.

FLEX IN THE U.S.

These common principles were developed first in the U.S. Air Force. Granted its independence from the U.S. Army in 1947, the air force flew into a decade of new technology and experimentation. Jets replaced piston engines and, with better radar and airframes, pilots were flying faster and higher than anyone ever thought possible. They just weren't doing it safely. In 1952, accidental deaths in the U.S. Air Force peaked at 1214—between three and four airmen killed every day. It was a disaster.

The U.S. Air Force started on a journey to limit that damage. They began to focus as much on human capabilities as on the aircraft. How many G-forces[1] could a pilot stand before he blacks out, or worse, 'G-LOCs' a phenomenon where the pilot loses consciousness? What could prevent that from happening? How much data could a single pilot handle from scanning instruments and radio? How much did he need? How could a pilot, wingman, co-pilot, navigator or WSO (Weapons system Officer) share and absorb that information to track and complete a mission? How rational were those mission plans given all these human factors? Gradually, these questions were answered. Slowly, in U.S.-based maneuvers and through the Korean War, accident rates fell.

Yet when it came to the crucible of the Vietnam War, it seemed the learning didn't count for much. If the answers were known, they weren't being taught to young pilots. Against the North Vietnamese, the U.S. Navy and Air Force were losing one aircraft for every 2.5 enemy planes shot down. That ratio may sound good but, given the superiority in technology and training, it was another disaster. In World War II and Korea, with more evenly matched technology, the ratio had been closer to one lost for every 10 shot down. Now they were losing two state-of-the-art multimillion-dollar F-4 Phantoms for five cheap old MiG-17 and MiG-21 Soviet planes.

Yet if a pilot survived their first few flights—a big if—they would survive for a very long time. Whatever they learned through experiencing those first flights made all the difference. So the challenge was clear: how could they transfer that learning to new pilots *before* they went into combat? The U.S. Air Force Fighter Weapons School, founded in 1949, was rapidly upgrading everything it could to meet that challenge, but more was needed for the Navy. In 1968, the Ault Report called for an institution that would intensively drill its pilots in everything they needed for aerial combat. It came in the form of the U.S. Navy Fighter Weapons School, dubbed 'Top Gun', and it rigorously taught mission planning and execution, briefing and debriefing, strategy and tactics. By the end of the Vietnam War in 1975, the combat kill ratio had been restored to 13 to 1.

Over the next 50 years, the U.S. fighter pilot schools drummed the principles of mission planning into their training, to improve their training, and to make flying in training and in combat safer. Eventually, the pilots of the U.S. Air Force could do what others could not, no matter the technical abilities of their planes. In 2002, the air force lost just nine airmen in accidents: 1214 down to just nine deaths, despite the variance in the types of plane, types of mission, and types of pilot.

These fighter pilot principles had no universally-accepted name, but they worked. These are the principles that Murph learned when first stationed at Luke Air Force Base in Arizona, and were taught at the U.S. Air Force Weapons School at Nellis Air Force Base, Nevada. They are the principles that the U.S. Marine Corps Weapons and Tactics Instructor course teaches at Yuma, Arizona, and that the U.S. Navy Strike Fighter Tactics Instructor program teaches its TOPGUN aspirants and graduates.

MURPH'S STORY

Murph hadn't planned to be a fighter pilot. Like many young kids he was aiming to be a professional athlete and, like most, just missed making the grade. His dad was a salesman, based in rural Kentucky selling IBM typewriters and then sets of World Book encyclopedias the old way, door-to-door. Every night, Murph listened to the day's personalities, conversations, and sales over the dinner table. So when professional baseball didn't make its long-awaited call after college, Murph started selling too, selling photocopiers with his dad. But two years later, he met a fighter pilot, and couldn't believe how keen that guy was to be what he was. That was a new course in life well worth charting.

Murph went all in too, for eight and a half years flying F-15s with the USAF, learning to think, to prepare, to fly, and then to teach other fighter pilots at Dobbins Air Force Base, Georgia, and later with the Florida Air National Guard. The whole time, he kept turning his mind to how those principles would translate to his old world, in sales and business. Four years in, he was asked to take business executives up in the air on incentives flights. One particularly rainy day the flight was called off and a group of executives were given a tour of the grounded F-15, a run in a flight simulator, and a talk from Murph on how his squadron pushed for flawless execution in their missions.

That was the first time Murph gave such a talk, and it made quite an impression. The CEO of the Conco Paint Company said he could use that sort of thinking, and would call in a year. A year later to the week the CEO called, and interviewed Murph to help run his sales division using the principles of flawless execution. To that time, the division's annual record was just over U.S.$5 million in sales. Two years later, they hit U.S.$52 million. Murph confirmed that everything he'd learned as a fighter pilot

Murph and the leadership team at Afterburner.

could be applied equally to his everyday business missions, and as much to his long-term plans. And Murph realized that his greatest asset was not what he was selling, nor even who he was. It was the way that he worked: the only way he knew how—using principles he began to call Flex.

Murph set up the consulting firm Afterburner Inc. in 1996 to share Flex with the business world. He used Flex every step of the journey, and continues to do so in ways that we'll discover in this book. Since then, Afterburner and its 70 fighter pilots and other elite military professionals have worked with over a thousand corporations and over 1.5 million people. Many of those pilots have launched their own businesses, and many more of Afterburner's clients have done the same. Flex works.

FLEX IN AUSTRALIA

Just as Murph was entering civilian life, the RAAF began to take a more serious interest in the principles that underpinned his training with the U.S. Air Force. There was much in common between the cultures of the two air forces—the openness, honesty, and accountability—but they were quite different in the way pilots operated and learned. The Australians were more like their UK Royal Air Force (RAF) colleagues. Yes, there were procedures, but they were more guidelines than orders. Yes, there was training, but that was more the school of hard knocks than rigorous, systematic induction.

The early 1990s changed all that. Put simply, too many pilots were losing their lives unnecessarily. Five Australian F/A-18A Hornet pilots died in the five years to 1992, the first years of the new plane's operation. For six years in a row the top-of-class U.S. fighter pilot who was selected to fly with the RAF on exchange, died by flying into low British hills. Both tragic and embarrassing, that record highlighted unacceptable training and combat safety in a period of higher than usual risks, including the use of Harrier jump jets that were four times more accident-prone than the Hornet.

Though forced now to look harder at the U.S. Air Force methods, the Royal Air Force still resisted. They looked at the USAF Fighter Weapons School approach, and were sceptical. It was too structured, with too much reliance on strict protocols and procedures for weapons engagement and communication which, the RAF believed, were too rigid and restrictive.

The Australians were less sceptical, more willing to learn from the best overseas. They understood that the standards and protocols just calmed down the pilots, took the pressure off thinking about the simple things, so that they could concentrate on the more dangerous things, their immediate mission, and risks. So the RAAF took on what they learned. Having to do better with their new Hornets, the RAAF's Fighter Combat Instructor (FCI) course adopted the principles of the U.S. Fighter Weapons School. Only they took them further. While the U.S. training was for nine weeks, the RAAF's spanned six months. It piled individual awareness and decision-making on top of regimented standards. Each week both of these schools pushed the pilots harder: more rapid planning, under more stressful conditions, on more complex missions, with more resources, and more threats. Each stage of planning and execution was ramped up until the FCI pilots could lead fighter squadrons with any air force, in any circumstances.

It also helped that these fighter pilot operational principles were consistent with those being used throughout the Australian military. The Joint Military Appreciation Process (JMAP) is used for joint campaign and operational planning within and across the Australian Defence Force. What is true for JMAP is true for Flex: 'Foremost in the minds of commanders should be that JMAP simply assists and promotes critical thinking rather than being an end in itself. It is not supposed to be used as a formulaic checklist that, once completed, will automatically provide the best solution to a problem. Creativity and flexibility of thought lie at the center, with the JMAP framework providing guidance and a measure of structure.'[2]

By the turn of the century, fighter pilots trained in the RAAF took on the operational cycle of plan–brief–execute–debrief, and all of the mission alignment, awareness, and execution principles that went with it. By that time also, the RAF was thinking the same way. So that in 2001, when Christian 'Boo' Boucousis became one of the few RAAF pilots accepted into an RAF Tornado fighter squadron, he found the operational approach as common as it could be to what he had learned in the RAAF.

BOO'S STORY

In 2005 Boo returned from a relatively uneventful mission, and was unable to move his head. At all. His neck had frozen, and took over a month to slowly remobilize. A series of tests revealed he had a rare degenerative medical condition: ankylosing spondylitis and osteoporosis. Stiff and softening bones weren't what the air force wanted in the front seat of a combat aircraft. Boo's fighter pilot career was over.

With that grim news, Boo spent months in a deep, dark space. It wasn't until he met a South African in similar circumstances in Britain, someone who knew what he was going through, that the first lights were turned on again. Boo was badly disillusioned by the fate of a non-combat injury dealing him out of the cockpit. Tom Naude was disillusioned with the British Army after a very challenging, heavy-combat tour in Iraq as a parachute regiment officer. They got to talking, and the talk led them to explore what they'd do next, and the decision to do whatever it was together. But what?[3]

Over the next eighteen months, Tom and Boo did little else but use their Flex-ability to plan the next phase in their lives. True to form, their initial thinking was simple and focussed: what business opportunities were they familiar with from their air force experience, and for which demand always outstripped supply? Anything, they reasoned, that supported military and humanitarian missions in Iraq and Afghanistan. And one of those two countries was too dangerous even for them.

To have a closer look at the options in Afghanistan, Tom took a position as security adviser to the United Nations for the 2004 national and provincial elections in Afghanistan. Western aid was pouring into the country, targeting essential infrastructure and services. Every piece of road, telecommunications, water, or energy works needed security. Tom and Boo decided that was the start they needed, and set up CTG Global. An American civil engineering firm needed protection for the headline Kabul to Kandahar road project, United States Agency for International Development's (USAID's) number one Afghan project. Boo and Tom found twenty Gurkhas for the job. Gurkhas are the fearless Nepalese soldiers who have served with distinction in the Nepalese, British, Indian, and Singapore armies for centuries.

Why Gurkhas? Because they understood military processes and character and the operating environment, and were willing, disciplined, and intelligent. It proved a great choice.

Soon after, CTG Global secured contracts with the UN donor program to protect school and medical clinic sites and manage their construction. The company began supplying people to other contractors—demand truly did outstrip supply in war-torn Afghanistan. It was dangerous work, and so the safety of their employees was paramount. CTG's safety record was second to none, and their reputation for it grew.

Nonetheless, eventually and perhaps inevitably, one of their Gurkhas was killed on duty. For young entrepreneurs in a foreign land, this was a critical test of who they were. They had seen how other contractors handled this situation, a lead they didn't want to follow. Rather, they wanted to demonstrate their respect for Sahi and his family to military standards, but without military or diplomatic support.

When Sahi died, Boo went to Kathmandu to personally visit the sixteen households who had lost a father, a brother, or a friend. As he did, Tom set about repatriating Sahi's body to Nepal so that he could be cremated by his family on the banks of the holy Bagmati River. But the custom in Afghanistan was and is burial the day after death, so there was no call or resources for preserving and transporting bodies. Tom had to track down formaldehyde in a Kabul pharmacy, teach himself the undertaker's crafts of embalmment and grooming, and make arrangements for preserving Sahi's body for its return to Nepal.

Doing the right thing is its own reward, but often brings unexpectedly positive effects. Word spread of Tom's efforts. Other contracting firms called on CTG to provide the same repatriation services for the many more workers who died on Afghan worksites. And many more Gurkhas sought out CTG Global for employment. Within a year of their first commission, CTG had 200 employees.

Within three years, they had 1600 men and women supporting humanitarian and infrastructure projects in the Middle East.

By any measure, this was an extraordinary achievement for two young men in their late twenties with no prior business experience. Yet for Boo and Tom, it was just Flex as usual, with a little extra grit and determination. Every step of the way, they applied what they knew from their military experience. That they had never worked together before, and had been in two different forces, mattered not one jot. Both the Royal Australian Air Force and the UK's Royal Air Force spoke the same language and operated in the same way—the same way as Murph's U.S. Air Force. They didn't call it Flex, but that's what it was and is.

We'll have a closer look at the CTG Global story throughout this book. We'll also learn about how Flex assisted Boo in another business: building the world's highest modular hotel, on time and on target.

Mode Developments' Perth hotel tops out at level 17, with all modules in place, on time and on target.

WHAT IS FLEX?

What just happened? What are we aiming for? How can we get there? Can we do it better? If any of these questions are on your mind, you've turned to the right page. Let's take stock of your situation.

Say you know what you're trying to achieve, but things aren't quite going to plan. There may be any number of reasons for that, but mostly it's because of one of these: the plan wasn't so good (assuming there was one), people didn't know their plan well enough, or they didn't execute it as planned.

If you met with your team and talked about it honestly, you'd be able to work out what fell short: the plan, the communication, or the execution. It can't really be anything else. You can point the finger at something else, but was that something you could have foreseen? And, if so, could you have dealt with it as part of your plan?

That conversation—'What just happened? or How are we doing?'—is where Flex usually starts. It's a review of an action, or a check-in on your progress. Someone, somewhere wants to have that conversation. We can't call it a debrief because, as we'll see, a debrief assumes there are a few things in place to begin with. But having that conversation will help make sure that next time you do something, you'll plan it better, brief it better, and execute it better.

FLEX GETS THINGS DONE

That's certainly how Afterburner helped the New York Giants, six games into the 2011–12 National Football League (NFL) season. With Eli Manning at quarterback, receiver Victor Cruz, Justin Tuck on defense, and a 4-and-2 record, the Giants weren't short of talent. But coach Tom Coughlin didn't see that talent delivering. They'd won the Super Bowl title four years earlier, but on form it wasn't going to happen again. The team sensed it, the coaching staff sensed it, and every game had a post-game review that was bringing out the worst in both. They were free-for-alls, with quite a bit of competition for who could shout 'We gotta do XYZ better!' the loudest. It was clear to everyone that if they were going to execute better on the field, they had to communicate better off the field.

The players turned to Afterburner to see if a more formal Flex debrief might work a little better. This was a big decision for them. The team's leading players decided to hold a 30-minute session after every game for the rest of the season, come what may. They held it on their own time, with no coaches allowed. The offensive team held a debrief, and the defensive team held their own. And, true to a Flex debrief, they were 'nameless, rankless'—you spoke your mind, whoever you were.

In the first couple of sessions, in a safe environment and with quite a lot baggage to unload, the debriefs were 'interesting'. Rightly or wrongly, players got things off their chests. But that brought things out into the open where the players could deal with them. And they dealt with them the right way.

Eli Manning led the offensive team debrief. 'I wasn't coaching anybody, I was just coaching myself, looking at what I needed to do better, and telling everybody. Then everybody would talk about what they needed to do to improve.'[1] 'It wasn't about calling people out,' recalls linebacker Mathias Kiwanuka. 'It was an opportunity to see everybody hold themselves accountable.'

Through the debriefs, the Giants learned from themselves what they had to do if they were going to make the Super Bowl again. They'd taken responsibility for their own performance, as individuals and as a team. They got better each week. The debriefs built up energy and purpose. Each player identified what they had to do better, very specifically, and what help they needed from others to do that. They supported each other to make that improvement, and to do so consistently. They were pushing as hard as they could for flawless execution.

The Giants were supposed to have a rough year, and it was far from clear sailing. They finished the regular season with only a 9-and-7 record. They'd ranked dead last of 32 NFL teams in rushing offense for the season. In fact, they were the first team in NFL history to reach the Super Bowl with a negative point differential (394 scored versus 400 against). But they'd got better all year, won four sudden-death playoffs in a row, and nailed it when it counted.

The Flex debrief was far from the only reason the New York Giants won Super Bowl XLVI, but it sure helped. The next season, three more NFL teams learned about Flex debriefs. Eli Manning's brother Peyton took the practice to the Denver Broncos. Today, debrief sessions across the NFL are very different to what they were in 2012. By 2015, Afterburner had addressed eleven NFL teams out of the nation's 24, in all of its eight conferences. Those teams finished the season filling the top two or three positions in each conference. And, we're proud to say, two of those teams slugged it out in the 2016 Super Bowl, with the Denver Broncos holding the Carolina Panthers at bay in Peyton Manning's NFL farewell.

Flex gets things done.

The NFL teams use of Flex is high profile, but typical. The debrief is a classic Flex process: simple yet deliberate, exhaustive yet efficient, direct yet empowering. And though the debrief is a common start, Flex is a lot more than that. Flex really is an end-to-end way of getting the right things done, well. It helps you set your objectives and ultimate destination, decide a path to reach them, and complete the actions along that path—even if the ground beneath you shifts. All the time, it is making you a better leader and follower, and helping you build a better team and a better outfit, whatever it is that you do.

All this is important. Getting things done these days is rarely easy. Sure we have more opportunities, but with them come greater expectations, responsibilities, and risks. We have more people to keep happy—all those 'stakeholders'—with more demands. We face more uncertainty, because the changes are more frequent, and bring with them things we've never encountered before. We need to build for the future, at the same time as delivering today. So it's harder to do the things that really matter to us, personally and professionally, and do them well.

We believe Flex will help you. The Flex framework for action is deliberately simple. But as you work with it, you'll find it sharpens your team's awareness, its bias to action, and its accountabilities. Each part of the Flex process instills a belief that the mission is on track, that each person has a clear and critical role, and that they will fulfill it.

BALANCING THOUGHT AND ACTION, AT SPEED

Flex is a way of thinking and a framework for action that helps you to do the right things well.

We use the term Flex because it is true to what it is: a way of working with the flexibility to handle the speed, complexity, and uncertainty of modern business, and still deliver what you need to. It helps us quickly assess our situation, make a decision, get things done, and keep doing them better. Flex is also short for <u>fl</u>awless <u>ex</u>ecution, which is what we're aiming for.

Don't be alarmed: we know that perfection is impossible to achieve. But reaching for it, using Flex principles, gets you closer and closer. The U.S. Navy Blue Angels fly seemingly immaculate displays 250 times a year, and use these principles each time to inch closer to flawless execution, or to understand how they inched away. They're in no doubt of the need to do that: 'You can never get complacent, take anything for granted because it's that day that something's going to come up and bite you.'[2]

The Blue Angels look at the Flex principles in two ways, and we invite you to do the same.

First, Flex is a framework for action: a series of simple processes that drive consistent and effective action in a complex environment. Set a purpose and vision, then plan–brief–execute–debrief to get there, relying on standards that every Blue will swear by. The Blues work methodically through those processes with the same discipline they use when they're in the air. It helps them create new routines, set the day's mission, put what they need in place, and fly the mission safely. You'll see what we mean in Chapter 3, 'The Flex framework for action'.

Yet Flex is also a way of thinking that promotes judgment throughout the framework for action. The Flex way of thinking balances direction and autonomy, speed and consideration, simplicity and dynamism, reliability and creativity, process and awareness. These are extremely valuable balances to have. They engage people, and overcome uncertainty and complexity. We'll explore how Flex does this in Chapter 4, 'The Flex way of thinking'.

Most importantly, the Flex way of thinking and the Flex framework for action support and develop each other, yin to yang. Besides being an engine for getting things done, the Flex framework for action is also an ideal way to learn the Flex balances and apply them in action. Besides balancing process and awareness, the Flex way of thinking ensures that the team gets the right things done, and improves the way it does them.

In fact, the Flex engine of plan–brief–execute–debrief continues to develop our thinking by matching the four ways in which adults learn best. In planning, we consider new things collaboratively and expansively, taking in outside advice, and *processing* those ideas as a specific, actionable course of action. In the brief, we *hear* the leader's synthesis of the plan, stressing elements of situational awareness that will make a difference to the mission. In executing the mission, we *experience* the very things that beforehand only existed in concept, in our minds. We add our own perspectives of the situation to our learning, direct experience rather than indirect. And in the debrief, we *review* those perspectives, learning from cause and effect, learning that two people can perceive the very same event quite differently, and how to reconcile those perceptions.

THE FLEX FRAMEWORK
FOR ACTION

It's important that we give you a single tight picture of the Flex framework from the start.

Figure 1: F-22 Raptor

Source: Afterburner Inc.

Yep, that's our picture. It's an F-22 Raptor, the world's most advanced fighter jet. The sight of it sends tingles down our spines. Flying a jet like these gives us an enormous sense of possibility and achievement, of pride and responsibility. We can't all fly a jet, but we can all put ourselves in that frame of mind.

Looking at this jet, three things stand out: the cockpit, the fuselage that houses the engine, and the wings. Trust us, we could talk all day about this jet, but let's focus on just those three things.

THE ENGINE

The heart of our jet is the Flex engine, a magnificent all-purpose workhorse that has been tested in every imaginable situation. Below is the engine of our F-22 Raptor. Below it, you see what it looks like when you look deep into the casing.

Figure 2: Flex engine

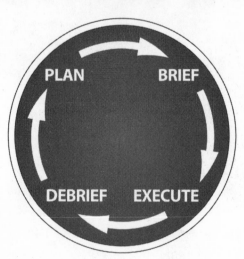

Source: Afterburner Inc.

Pretty simple? Good. We like simple. Our engine is the plan–brief–execute–debrief cycle. Each stage is finely tuned to get the best from your team. The more you run this cycle, the more powerful your engine will be, the better your team will run.

THE COCKPIT

The Flex engine has power to deliver, but if there's something missing in the cockpit, that power will go to waste. It needs purpose and guidance. That's you in the cockpit. It's your team, your mission, your accountability. And to fulfill your mission, as shown in Figure 3, you'll have three things in place: a high-definition vision of your destination (HD Destination), a clear course of action to get there, and a keen awareness about what is going on around you (situational awareness). If any of these elements are rusty or missing, your mission may well miss its mark.

Figure 3: Flex cockpit

Source: Afterburner Inc.

THE WINGS

Those smooth things off to the side that stay quiet hardly get a mention—want to try flying without them? For Flex, our wings are the standards we set for our processes and communication, and the training we hone to meet these standards. Not only do wings keep us airborne, they keep us steady at speed and through turbulence. As basic as they seem, we don't get far without our wings: see Figure 4.

Figure 4: Flex wings

Source: Afterburner Inc.

So that's our model for Flex. Put it all together, it looks like Figure 5.

Figure 5: The F-22 model of Flex

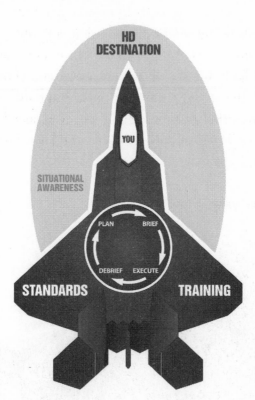

Source: Afterburner Inc.

Flex provides the framework for any significant actions we take: in business, in our professional lives, and even in our personal lives. Some of these actions may be quite short-term missions with tight objectives that we can complete in a day, a week, or a month. Others are long-term stretching over months or sometimes years. Yet we use the same flexible framework, asking the same questions and relying on the same disciplines to get the job done.

That's possible because our jet does not fly by itself. We are flying it, and we bring with us a way of thinking that balances opposites in a simple way while promoting good judgment. Flex is a team approach, with the team having a clear leader for each mission. The Flex way of thinking is disciplined enough to drive our performance and execution. That's what this book is about.

Nor are we flying alone. What we're aiming for is a team sharing the same framework for action and the same way of thinking. If they're flying with purpose as part of a larger organization, they're all aiming for the same HD Destination with a clear strategy to get there.

That's the way we like to think of our Flex framework. We can also present it diagrammatically, like this:

Figure 6: The pyramid model of Flex

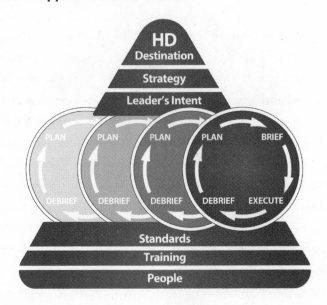

Source: Afterburner Inc.

How does our pyramid work? Everything starts and relies on your people. When they start in your organization, they get the training they need to know the standards they'll need to meet. Then they're ready to be part of an execution team: to plan, brief, execute, and debrief with the best of them. Their mission plan will meet their team leader's intent by employing the organization's strategy, helping it to reach its HD Destination. That's a whole lot of Flex language. But don't worry, we'll make it very clear as we go.

OK, we've introduced the Flex framework that guides the rest of this book. You have a choice: continue reading to learn why the Flex engine works, or go straight to Chapter 7, 'The six-step mission planning process', to start working your engine immediately—you can always come back when you'd like to.

Night scramble

Shortly after 9/11, with my squadron in the Colorado Air National Guard still on high alert, in the deepest part of my sleep the claxon went off at an ear-breaking decibel that had me flying out of bed and into the cold night air. Before I could even rub my eyes I was airborne, taking off in pursuit of my flight lead, 'heading west' as our only initial instruction. The briefing—or the 'nine-line' as we call it—would soon follow. It took less than ten minutes to get from a dead sleep to intercepting an airliner in the dead of night. The airliner was not squawking the correct code—the code given to the pilots by the air-traffic controllers to identify themselves. It was our job to intercept that liner and make sure they were not under duress.

It's nothing short of bizarre to find yourself waking up at 400 knots, wearing night-vision goggles in a single-seat fighter—much like a weird dream. The fact that we could go from unconscious to 400 knots over the mountains in the dark without any instructions other than 'go in a westerly vector' is thanks in large part to flawless execution. I'd never scrambled from a dead sleep to a full-blown intercept before, but I had prepared for this possibility. We had planned, briefed and trained for this potential scramble scenario. The plan was sitting 'on the shelf' in the back of our minds waiting to be pulled out at the moment it was needed. Not just us but the whole team, from the command post telling us the right details at the right time, to the maintenance team who had prepared our jets ahead of time and also got out of bed at the dead of night, to the team many states away at Western Air Defense sending the original scramble order and follow-on briefing. It took that entire team to plan ahead, prepare and train for this sort of scenario to occur.

So often in business, we see companies planning without the involvement of their lower ranks, without representation from the field. So often those plans fail because every aspect of the mission hasn't been considered. Teams that utilize true open planning to the full extent are able to incorporate all their wingmen into the process, increasing everyone's situational awareness, providing maximum flexibility in even the most complicated of scenarios.

'JackieO'¹

THE FLEX WAY OF THINKING

The Flex framework for action is very compelling, but it is the Flex way of thinking that makes it powerful: a series of balances that keep our action on target. As we've said, Flex balances direction and autonomy, speed and consideration, simplicity and dynamism, reliability and creativity, process and awareness. The combination of clear, simple processes and constructive ways of thinking allows you to take on the following three major challenges that can make it hard to achieve a team's goals:

1. **Flex engages people** by giving clarity to their roles, ownership of their plans, and accountability for their actions. Our economy and the people who work in it are changing. The economy is de-materializing, shifting from things being made to interesting ideas being shared. People are more educated, as they need to be to generate the ideas and the means to share them. As we will see, it is not enough for people who entered the workforce this century just to

be told to do things. These millennials need to know why. They need to know they have support. Flex answers these needs.

2. **Flex takes on uncertainty and complexity** with disciplined, collaborative processes. All those new ideas are mounting up. Whatever business we're in, we face more disruptive technologies, more regulations, and more competition. No one person can keep on top of all that. People are anxious, curious, distracted, overconfident. Given the speed of change and the complexity of our environment, there are more ideas, possibilities, initiatives, and challenges coming at us all the time. Some people are better than others at keeping focus. We need to open up our thinking to a broader awareness. But we need to do so in a simple, disciplined way, so that the focus is on the substance and not the process.

3. **Flex takes on the speed of change** with a strong bias towards getting things done and a short learning cycle. Ideas now spread immediately through our personal and public media, so change is occurring literally at the speed of light. That does not mean we should respond to everything instantly. We need to act in a considered way, but quickly. Flex provides the means to do so, and to keep learning from our actions.

These three Flex qualities work both for your creative strategies and for continually improving your core operations. They appear through every Flex process. Starting with your Flex planning—be it for shorter or longer missions—they carry right through the briefing, execution, and debrief stages of the Flex cycle, and strengthen the Flex wings.

A fighter pilot mindset only goes so far

As part of the Flex way of thinking, we'd like to clarify something. You won't be surprised to read that we deeply believe in the discipline and awareness that we learned flying jets as part of a combat squadron. We and our colleagues have relied on what we learned becoming second nature in all our endeavors—in the air force and other elite forces, in business, and in our personal lives—and the Flex process has allowed us to achieve our goals.

We've also appreciated how young men and women have been able to join our air forces with limited life experience, and get along. Yet we've had enough experience in business to know that life on the street, in the factory, in the boardroom and in our work teams is not the military. Which is perhaps a good thing.

The biggest difference of all between military and civilian life is that our important personal and business efforts are primarily *social* efforts. We are social animals. In anything we do we must be aware of and deal with the personal motivations and responses of our own family or team, and also the people they have to deal with. That's why we stress that Flex doesn't mean to 'act like a fighter pilot' in some boys-to-men dream of how the world works. In the military, engaging with the enemy is one step removed from this social world. By the time our fighter squadrons are called in, we're no longer negotiating with the enemy. We've stepped outside the sphere of human interactions, and into one where we rarely if ever even see the faces of our enemies.

When we moved from the military to negotiating business deals with governments, we realized how much we had to learn about human motivations and behavior. As first-class fighter pilots and squadron leaders, we understood how to work with and lead other fighter pilots. But we'd be the first to admit that that's a pretty narrow field of experience. Despite the thankfully growing number of female pilots, most fighter pilots are Type-A males, treating their teammates as they would other Type-A males. In life and in business, we're working with Type-A to Type-D males and Type-A to Type-D females, any one of whom may be the key to getting our dreams fulfilled. We've had to learn, as social animals, that building a workable, working, and social relationship with people is critical. That takes a different kind of wisdom and patience than what we mastered in an F/A-18 cockpit.

Nonetheless, every major effort we've made in our personal and business lives confirms for us the value of the disciplines we learned in the air force. The combination of operational discipline and emotional intelligence is extremely powerful. We are continuing to learn how one can build on the other. This book represents a large part of that learning. All its passages should reflect that awareness. If they don't, we're sure you'll let us know!

ENGAGING PEOPLE IN THEIR OWN MISSION

Engagement is one of the most overused words in the modern business lexicon. It isn't the answer to everything, but it remains powerful. For people to perform at anywhere near their best, they need to be 'engaged'. This is particularly true of millennials, the generation born from 1980 to 2000, who will comprise 50 percent of the global workforce by 2020.[1] To engage millennials, and in our view anyone else, you need to be both direct and empowering. That's how we were treated when in the air force, when we felt the whole organization supported us. Let us explain.

Skill, will, and autonomy

The machine metaphor works pretty well here. For a person to perform well, they need two personal gear cogs to be fully engaged: their *ability* to do something and their *desire* to do that thing. It's the simple skill–will matrix, and you want the people in your team to be moving towards the top right box (see Figure 7).[2]

Figure 7: The skill–will matrix

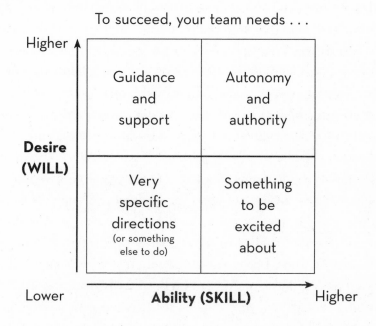

Source: The skill–will matrix is a common management tool, but this version from Dan Spira (©2010, danspira.com) captures it well.

Take a moment to think where the New York Giants were. This was a team that had won the Super Bowl four years earlier. They had skill in spades. The will? You'd like to think that if professional football players who are paid millions don't have the desire to win their championship, there's a real problem. They do. But they have to have it *more* than the other 31 teams in the competition. Manning, Cruz, Tuck & Co had tasted victory once, and thought they had one last shot at it. They wanted it.

You don't have to look long at the figure above to see what might have been missing. With a coaching staff of eighteen under head coach Tom Coughlin, there's no doubt the players had guidance, support, and perhaps some very specific directions. But the Flex debrief helped them develop the autonomy and authority they needed as the team on the field.

If your team has the skill and the will, then it needs its share of autonomy. Whether your team has autonomy or has to achieve it, whether you take autonomy or are given it, doesn't matter. Without it, you will not perform to your potential. At every stage of the Flex process (but one, as we'll see), teams take ownership for their mission's outcomes. Sure, they're given the direction and support they need, but they share the autonomy and authority to get the job done.

So far so good. Being a part of a team that wants and needs autonomy and authority, whether as leader or not, is where you want to be. People need the belief that what they're doing matters, and that they have some control over their actions. The big question then becomes—how much control? How much autonomy? We'll get into that more deeply when we discuss Flex planning (Chapter 6). For now we'll leave you with a quote that rings the bell for us:

> 'Don't tell people how to do things. Tell them what to do, and let them surprise you with the results.'
>
> General George S. Patton

Building skill and will

Sometimes even professional sportspeople lack the skill and will to excel at their level of competition. In fact, it can be pretty hard to maintain the desire to win week after week over a long season. We all have bad days—a champion golfer who cannot sink a putt for love or money is a familiar, often agonising sight on the circuit. It's easy to see why so many sports professionals employ a sports psychologist, someone who can help them focus on what they have to do.

It's easier still to be needing more will or more skill in our daily lives. No matter how much you love your vocation, sometimes getting to Friday can be a herculean task, when church or bar can't come soon enough. There are times when you lose all sense of timing in the calls you make and the lines you have to say. But in business, few of us have or want the luxury of a sports psychologist. 'Just a minute boss, I need a moment with Sigmund to help me get ready for this workshop' is not a line you want to try too often. It's usually up to you and your team.

Flex is designed to support you in having both the skill and the will to get the job done. The Flex process ensures that your team has the required range of skills—they learn the standards and receive the training they need to contribute through the Flex cycle, and it prioritizes keeping their skills sharp. Flex gives people the incentive to develop their own specialist techniques to do their job better. And Flex provides clear, reliable, and consistent processes to use to ensure that those individual skills are applied as a team—a skilled team.

Flex will help you and your team members to stay engaged in your mission, and give you the will to do your best. The culture that we've seen work time after time is pretty simple: be honest, answer 'why?' for people, give them clear roles and ownership for how they should fulfill their roles, and make them accountable. Everything about Flex is geared for that millennial culture, to generate and maintain the desire to perform. We've never met a fighter pilot who didn't have buckets of desire when they started. A trainee pilot is up for anything, ready to do anything for the opportunity to fly in their desired squadron. But it can be hard to maintain this will, and they can experience the same low points of any career. The Flex way of thinking helps bring them back on target.

Leadership and followership

You can't have a leader without followers. That makes both roles equally important. Being engaged is not one-way traffic, an expectation that someone has to engage you. It's something you have to bring to the party. The team won't work without your curiosity, and your willingness to follow, to contribute, to share possibilities and warnings. Flex assumes that each member of the team has a shared leadership role, and will soon be leading their own team. Team members are taking part in many of the processes that make for good leadership, and learning those ropes. Most importantly, they are supporting their leader in their own learning and practice, by helping to build respectful truth over artificial harmony (see Chapter 5, 'The respectful truth of a Flex team').

Every element of Flex is designed to fully switch on the people responsible for getting the job done. The four stages of the Flex engine make sure this happens by ensuring team members: think collaboratively (Plan), are personally charged to act (Brief), enjoy mutual support (Execute), and experience deliberate review (Debrief).

BEATING COMPLEXITY WITH A CLEAR, COLLABORATIVE PROCESS

If 'engagement' is an overused word these days, then 'complexity' is right up there with it. And for good reason: it's a lot better than

'VUCA', which is what a lot of military types use to cover the volatility, uncertainty, complexity, and ambiguity that's actually going on. If change has always been with us, the telling points now are the *speed* and *novelty* of the changes, and the *uncertainty* of whether and how they will happen: we just don't know what will happen because we've never had these technologies before.

We argue that to perform well in a complex environment—that is, to solve problems, make decisions, plan, execute, and learn— you need the *disciplined, collaborative process of a diverse, aware group.* Let's take a look at those elements.

A diverse, aware group

While Flex works for individuals, it is designed to get the best out of teams. Because to take on complexity, one person is rarely enough. Edgar Schein, the father of organizational culture from MIT, puts it this way: in a complex environment 'managers as individuals no longer know enough to make decisions and get things done.'[3] They need a team, and for the team to do their job well.

There are too many traps for an individual to fall into, in both planning and performing. These are the cognitive errors that we mere mortals keep making day after day. We are optimistic by nature and, research suggests, systematically overconfident. Can we build it? Yes we can, no matter what the facts say. If we've already invested time and effort, then we'll spend even more to get our job done, ignoring advice to cut our losses.

What evidence do we hold onto to support these decisions? That's when we toss objectivity aside. We reach for data that supports our hunches, and downplay the rest. We hold up our personal experience as indubitable proof, far more powerful than what thousands of others may have seen or done. And data from yesterday has to be more relevant than data from last year, right? The Nobel Prize-winner Daniel Kahneman's catch-all book *Thinking Fast and Slow* takes us though any number of biases we rely on to make poor decisions in the face of contrary evidence.[4]

That's why the so-called 'wisdom of crowds' has more going for it than the average bar stool theory. James Surowiecki's book *Wisdom of Crowds* pulls up the classic example of the jar of jelly-beans at the school fete.[5] He cites finance professor Jack Treynor running the experiment in his class. The average of 56 guesses was pretty close to the mark: 871 beans against 850 in the jar. But only two guesses out of the 56 beat that average. So you want to believe that you'll be one of that pair if you want to beat the average.

So it makes sense for a team to get together to work out how best to pull off an important mission. What then if everyone in the team had the same background and skills, and thought the same? We're a bit nervous when it comes to talking about diversity. There is no doubting that fighter pilots are not the most diverse group of people on earth, and equally that our training draws our thinking and actions even more tightly together. Within the bounds of our fighter pilot circles, we do push to call on as diverse a group as possible for our ground and air missions, and in Chapter 10, 'Corner speed', you'll meet a RAAF team that deliberately included people who were 'outlier' personalities within the force.

To demonstrate why, consider the example that Scott Page uses in *The Difference*, a book that shows how our collective wisdom is greater than the sum of what we know individually.[6] Imagine that you're hiring to fill two positions in your team, and you're down to three candidates who you can't decide between: Bob, Sue, and John. You decide that a simple ten-question test will help you make the final call. Sue scores 7, John 6, and Bob 5. Problem solved? Not quite. What if these were their actual scores?

	Q1	Q2	Q3	Q4	Q5	Q6	Q7	Q8	Q9	Q10	
Sue	✓	✓			✓	✓	✓		✓	✓	7
John	✓	✓				✓	✓		✓	✓	6
Bob			✓	✓	✓			✓	✓		5

Choosing Sue and John would give you the same way of thinking twice over. Choosing Bob and Sue, or even Bob and John, would give you a broader point of view. Those pairings will give you greater cognitive diversity, which is what you want in your team. Diversity can offer any number of perspectives, across gender, age, technical expertise, education, personality type, ethnicity, social interests—anything that can offer your team an alternative view of similar facts. We talk further about the makeup of your team in Chapter 5, 'The Flex team', but if you want to perform well through complexity, you want diversity on your team.

Creativity through a disciplined process

With all that diversity, you can expect differing opinions on how to act, and how to begin that action. That's where a disciplined process comes in. A process like Flex brings diverse ideas to a common objective focus. At each stage of the process, there are clear questions being asked, and clear answers being sought. The source of those answers doesn't matter, objectivity does. It's like making a strong cable out of thin wires. The process laces the diverse strands of facts and opinion together into one strong plan of action.

It's hard to overstate the power of a disciplined process. In a 2010 study, McKinsey & Company analyzed everything a company did in making decisions that affected performance—performance being measured by revenue, profitability, market share, and productivity.[7] Everything could be put into three categories: the data (raw company, market, or industry data); the data analysis and modelling; and the processes used to exploit that analysis and make decisions. Which of the three had the greater impact on performance? McKinsey found that performance was determined 39 percent by the quality of the data, just 8 percent by the quality of the analysis, and 53 percent by the quality of the decision processes. That's right, the decision process has over six times the impact as the analysis it's based on!

That research really rams home the point that teams and companies often overplay data analysis. The research explains why we often suffer from 'analysis paralysis', spending more time than we should on analysis, and delaying the decisions we need to make. Perhaps it's because analysis is the easiest thing to do, and the one thing that business analysts are trained to do well. Getting accurate data is hard. Making good decisions is harder.

Making good decisions *consistently* is harder still. We're as much of a fan of Jim Collins as anyone. In *Great by Choice*, Collins writes that 'the signature of mediocrity is not an unwillingness to change: the signature of mediocrity is chronic inconsistency'.[8] That's again where a reliable process comes in—to drive consistent quality in your decisions and actions.

People sometimes misunderstand processes, and give them a bad rap. The objections are that they're a straitjacket, that they stifle creativity, that they take the fun out of work. Bad processes can do that. Good processes don't. As Jim Collins calls it: 'The great task, rarely achieved, is to blend creative intensity with relentless discipline so as to amplify the creativity rather than destroy it.'[9]

Are pilots concerned about creativity? Not so much. Are we concerned about the creativity of our clients? Very much so. We know creativity is a necessary ingredient of their success.

But we are more concerned about our clients' productivity and working culture. A good process such as Flex does one big thing to help enormously: it reduces friction. In every meeting, people know what they're aiming to do, and how they will do it. It saves a heck of a lot of time, a heck of a lot of argument, and a great many working relationships. People may have different personalities and different world views. They may not even like each other. But they can work together with a clear, disciplined, collaborative process.

BEATING THE SPEED OF CHANGE WITH A BIAS TO ACTION

It's a safe bet that the pace of business is not going to slow down any time soon. It's speeding up on whatever measure you choose: product cycles, technology adoption, market volatility, emergence of competition. The classic example is that it took 45 years for telephones to reach 50 percent of the US population, and just five years for cellphones to do the same.[10] The automotive design cycle has tightened from five years to two to three years over the past decade. But digital services—the smartphones and apps we now rely on to order pizzas, do our banking, and monitor our heart rate—make a joke of these cycle times. The speed these apps are being developed and launched means that a market opportunity must be exploited yesterday, or not at all.

Hence the belief that it's wiser to act now with an 80 percent plan, than to launch a perfect plan when it's too late. Anne Mulcahy is the former CEO and chairman of Xerox and now on the boards of Citigroup, Johnson & Johnson, and the *Washington Post*. While at Xerox, Mulcahy learned the cost of being 'risk averse, and too data driven. By the time we would reach a decision that some technology was going to be a home run, it had either already been bought or was so expensive we couldn't afford it'. So now she's a believer that, 'Decisiveness is about timeliness. And timeliness trumps perfection. The most damaging decisions are the missed opportunities, the decisions that didn't get made in time.'[11] Figure 8 is one interpretation of how value gets crushed by delay, as the competition jumps in and then the market itself moves on.

Figure 8: The time value of action

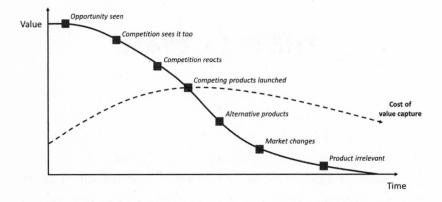

Source: Redrawn and adapted from John A. Warden III and Leland A. Russell, *Winning in Fast Time*.[12]

So nothing is surer or more clichéd than that we're in a complex, uncertain, fast-moving world. The choice is to sit like a rabbit in the headlights, or to act. Flex is designed to help you act when you can't know everything you'd like to. When pilots prepare a mission, we're told when the mission has to take place. The start time isn't a variable. Flex helps us to deal with that time constraint in three ways: preparing for the mission in a rigorous but *finite* process, responding to the situation during the mission, and capitalizing on a short learning cycle before the next, inevitable mission.

5

THE FLEX TEAM

It's hard to imagine a serious endeavor that is not taken on by a team. Every person that does something special and 'solo' is the first to recognize the team behind them. Matt Hall is one of Australia's finest modern pilots, having served in the RAAF for eighteen years before becoming a standout performer in the Red Bull Air Race. A solo pilot, yes, but it takes a team of eight to put him into the air. When Paralympic champion Kurt Fearnley took on the infamous Kokoda Track in Papua New Guinea, without his wheelchair—literally crawling over the trail—he had a team behind him. The entrepreneurial celebrities of our times—Steve Jobs, Mark Zuckerberg, Elon Musk, Oprah, Richard Branson, Bill Gates, Jeff Bezos, Lucy Peng, John Mackey, Anita Roddick, Herb Kelleher, Diane von Furstenberg, Muhammad Yunus, Howard Schultz, Arianna Huffington, Larry Page, Sergey Brin, Fred Smith—all acknowledge their greatest achievement as being the team they put in place to realize their dreams.

Good teams don't happen by accident. There are a series of decisions to be made, on the team's makeup, its culture, and the way it makes decisions and gets things done. Flex teams have to have a good leader, but equally they have to have good followers, sharing the same purpose and vision, and able to step into the leader's shoes at any point, which at some point they will.

WHO IS FLEX FOR?

Teams are those groups of around five to twelve people who share a common mission. They are big enough to have the skills and diversity the mission needs, and small enough for each team member to know and rely on each other, and to care about each other. Selection, training, and shared experience allow team members to appreciate the culture, standards, and processes that enable the team to work. They are different people, with different personalities, perspectives, and life values, but what they do share is a common purpose, a desire to achieve that purpose, and mutual trust.

The teams we'll meet in this book share those team attributes, but are extremely diverse in makeup. They can be small, independent teams; one of many similar teams in a large organization; or a large organization itself. Surgical teams have been using Flex with incredible results, dramatically improving on their hospital's average performance on some key metrics. Sports teams can be entire operations, like the New York Giants or Denver Broncos, or separate units within the team: the offense, defense, and special teams.

This book focusses on Flex teams in business, though it uses examples from other fields. We'll meet leaders of companies who have used Flex to set and achieve a common purpose. We'll also meet small teams that have quite focussed roles within a corporation: construction teams, maintenance crews, sales teams, product launch teams, bakers, truckers . . . and everything in between.

CREATING A FLEX TEAM

What's important for now is that almost any group of people can become a Flex team. Why? Because Flex helps you create that team. Flex is all about creating a common purpose, about creating desire and confidence, about creating trust. It's about your role in that team—be it as a clear team leader or as an essential follower—in creating a team that performs its mission, consistently and reliably, every time.

That's a challenge. There are many components to a team, and many things that can go wrong. We've cut the idea of a Flex team a million times over from every which way we can, and it boils down to these three things: the team's mindset, its skillset, and the processes that bring those two together. When you define these three things, you define your team.

Your hand-picked team

Startup companies are in many respects the new classic team. Small, nimble, focussed—and hand-picked by the company's founders. They have to succeed to get paid, and can't rely on a corporate machine to generate bonuses. Technology startups can amaze with the speed with which they take hold of an idea, and spread it through our digital lives. Equally impressive though are new companies that take on the traditional market for physical goods. Kill Cliff is one of those.

Kill Cliff is the brainchild of Todd Ehrlich, a retired Navy SEAL who thought there must be a better alternative to sugar-, motrin-, and caffeine-laden drinks after his daily workouts. Among the many things Todd learned in the navy, besides how to take out a target, was that gut inflammation caused more health issues than most people would want to know, and that electrolytes helped manage inflammation as well as workout recovery. Surely there was something he could do with that.

The drinks market has to be one of the most crowded markets on the planet, dominated by the behemoths of PepsiCo and The Coca-Cola Company and the brands they own. If you want to take that market on, you want to be smart about it, have a great team working with you, and work harder than you thought possible. Kill Cliff took on that challenge, sold its first case of anti-inflammatory recovery drink in 2012 and, so far, is winning in a ridiculously tough market.

From the outset, Todd moved on the three things that mark out a team: mindset, skills, and process. Like all good teams this one had a clear mindset of identity and purpose: to build a market for Kill Cliff, a new product with something to offer. If Kill Cliff didn't sell, no one got paid. For the team's skillset, Todd followed the Navy SEAL rule for team recruiting. In SEAL platoons, at least two men can do any task, and each man has to have at least two specialities. 'One is none, and two is one,' is a spec ops saying, and Kill Cliff would take it on. The first team would have diverse but overlapping skills. They could cover for each other, and test out their ideas. People had accountability, but support.

To keep the team's mindset responsive and its skillset sharp, Kill Cliff used the Flex cycle in fast mode. Every day, Todd and his team tested and reset their plans. It may only have taken five minutes, but they had to keep their edge, because every step they took tested their ingenuity and resistance. Retailers had seen it all before and were sceptical. Competitors fought back. The situation quickly became more dynamic than they had imagined. Payment terms, product returns, shelf-space—everything had to be thought, re-thought, and re-negotiated every day.

The team you've just got to work with

That's all very well when you're able to pick your own team—pick who has the skills, who'll get along, who loves the mission. But it's a different story when the team is already picked, and the mission is upon you. That's what we faced working with the resource giants Santos and BHP Billiton on their offshore oil rigs in the Timor Sea.

Our objective was to improve safety on the offshore rigs, massive structures that can stand over 600 feet (200 metres) high and withstand 90-knot winds and 60-foot (20-metre) waves. To improve safety, you have to improve processes. For the processes we're dealing with, people had been flown in from all over the world. We had specialists from the rig owners, from the companies hiring the rigs, from the rig operators Diamond Offshore, from specialists such as Haliburton for concreting the drill bits, and various other sub-specialists and contactors. On top of it all, we had four crews of 90 people each from all over Australia, hired through an employment agency, with little in common except the skills and desire to earn good money living on an oil rig for a fortnight on and a fortnight off.

All of these agencies had their own management systems and cultures, and their own ways of operating an oil rig. We were called in to help meld those cultures and processes together, so that the teams could operate the rigs collaboratively. These crews already had their skills, they had their own versions of an offshore rig culture, and they had their own idea of process. Good operators they were. Teams they weren't.

The only lever we had to work with was process. We were outsiders—who were we to start talking about culture? But the processes we had were solid. We used the disciplines of briefing and debriefing to form these crews into solid, effective teams.

Each person on the rigs had been briefed to do their job, and had signed long documents agreeing that they knew their job and took responsibility for their safety. They were used to daily 'toolbox talks' too, start-of-day team talks that pointed everyone to the day's work. But they weren't used to Flex briefs and debriefs.

The Flex briefs were prepared the night before by a planning team with representatives of all the rig's agencies. The day's objectives were agreed, the threats identified, and the plans set. The morning's briefs were absolutely of the moment. Safety was no longer something to hear a lecture on, it was part of the here and now. The day's actions and contingencies were laid out, for that site, on that day, in those conditions. Between those briefings and the operator's own skills, there was nothing academic, nothing irrelevant, and nothing left to imagine. At the end-of-day debriefing, the teams identified new steps to make the processes safer and more effective. Those steps became new standards. Slowly, as the teams' shared processes took shape, the teams' shared culture did too. The learning was clear to those involved: use Flex as the process to meld both the processes and culture.

Teams that make up organizations

As we've said, one of the most valuable traits of the Flex approach is that it is designed to be used both in small teams and in very large organizations: the 307,000 people in the U.S. Air Force, for example. If that's a little too large to wrap your head around, try one of the U.S. aircraft carriers that Navy jets and pilots live on. Each carrier has around 5000 crew, almost all aged between nineteen and 21. Every three years, every aspect of that carrier is renewed, including its crew. On that 36-month rotation, the entire boat gets re-fitted for another ten-month mission, and 90 percent of its crew will be entirely new. They've just been on another ship on another mission, and just slip right into the new one. And yet the mission gets executed all but flawlessly. That's because every person on that ship has a clear understanding of how they will work together, using Flex-like principles.

This is the understanding you are likely to have to build in your own organization, big or small. We no longer stay in one position for our entire worklife, nor a single organization, nor even a single career. (Millennials are changing careers every five years, changing jobs every two-and-a-quarter years—about half the current average terms for all workers in the U.S.)[1] People will come and go, and be your friends and colleagues in other ways. You need a simple approach for the people who join your organization to become one of your team.

THE RESPECTFUL TRUTH OF A FLEX TEAM

It's not easy to create such teams. Not because the processes or principles are hard to understand, but because we find them hard to commit to and stand by. A Flex team cares for and respects each other, starting with the leader's care for the rest. For their professional time and goals, team members share a common culture and purpose. The phrase that rings throughout their experience is 'Respectful truth over artificial harmony'. Flex teams do not gloss over the difficult, just to be polite or avoid conflict. But they manage these situations with respect, because they have the clear processes to deal with them, and learn to do so.

People who care

As we will see, respectful honesty is called for most in debriefing a situation that has not gone well, when the temptation to point blame and undermine people is at its greatest. That's why the debrief works through a process that focusses on determining the actions taken and their causes. That's why there's a very real distinction between an accidental error, which is human and readily forgettable, and a deliberate breach of a mission plan or standards, which is a violation of trust. That's why people own up to their own mistakes, because they feel the responsibility of honesty to each other. They care. People feel vulnerable, and it is up to the leader to set that tone, to put him or herself in a vulnerable position first, by being the first to own up to their mistakes. Because the leader cares most.

How do you make that care real, rather than just a word? There are many examples we can share from our business experience. 'Serge' talks about having to find a half million dollars in headcount savings. It would have been easy, as many firms do, to just cut those with the poorest performance record, or in roles that are losing their priority. Instead, Serge went through his whole division to ask and find out what individuals *needed*, for themselves and their families. Some were breadwinners, some were near-retirees, some were starting out. They all understood the situation, and they all worked through the problem. It took a week, and the HR budget was halved as it had to be. Everyone got what they needed. Not everything they wanted, perhaps, but wherever they ended up, it was in a good place.

That's the type of care that Flex creates. Leaders who pull out all stops to mark occasions that need marking, who don't just place a phone call to order a turkey for the folks working on Christmas Day, but cook and carve it for them. They go out on a limb and take risks for their team because they care. Perhaps it's because fighter pilots are taught from the outset that they're the most valuable thing in the air, no matter what their jet cost. The plane can be replaced, they cannot. That assurance carries over to the way they treat each other. Despite the forceful personalities in it, a squadron is not the bear pit of egos you see in *Top Gun*, fun though it is to imagine.

Shared culture and desire

If you walk into a room of fighter pilots, you know you're mixing with a team. We may not be the team you want to mix with, we may not float everyone's boat, but that's not the point. We know who we are, and what we're here for.

That's no accident. The USAF and the RAAF both spend

enormous amounts of time and energy selecting people who had not just the skills but the attitudes and culture they believe they can rely on. Murph saw it when he was finishing his F-15 training at Luke Air Force Base in Arizona, eighteen months into the Air Force. Each classmate had a different background, from a different part of the country, with a different style of education. But they dreamed the same things, respected the same strengths, laughed at the same jokes, drank the same beer, talked in similar patterns, had almost identical mannerisms. Most chewed gum the same way. The same type of gum.

You would get the same impression in a room of the U.S. Army's 5th Ranger Battalion. Back on D-Day, 6 June 1944, General Norman Cota stormed along Omaha Beach in Normandy amid shells and gunfire, looking to drive the American troops inland from their beachhead. He came across a group looking more intent than most. 'What unit are you with?' he screamed over the noise. 'Fifth Rangers,' one replied. 'Well then,' said the general, 'lead the way!'

From that day forward, 'Rangers lead the way!' has been the battlecry of one of the most respected special ops forces in the world. Every soldier bearing the arched yellow and black Ranger tab on his uniform has passed through the Ranger Assessment and Selection Program (RASP) at Fort Benning, Georgia. Every year another intake of 350 to 400 qualified soldiers face the RASP, and only 250 make it to the fourth day. A select number of the RASP intake will later attend Ranger School, the combat leadership course that is the toughest two months the U.S. Army has yet devised, a wall and swamp torture test that takes an average of 35 pounds or 16 kilos off every surviving Ranger. It's sleep depriving, mentally draining, and physically brutal.

But there's a point to it all. The survivors have shown they have the intelligence, mental toughness, personal courage, motivation, and discipline to be part of the 75th Ranger Regiment, the modern successor to the wartime 5th Battalion. They're the qualities they want in the culture they've created. The successful soldiers may have such qualities at levels most of us will never need. This is all in the 'Do not try this at home' category, but they're good qualities to have.

None of this was a birthright. The Rangers took people who might make the grade, and got them there through a process. The same as the USAF's process can put very young men behind the stick of U.S.$35 million warplanes. You've seen it in *The Right Stuff*, the film about Chuck Yeager and the test pilots of Project Mercury on a mission to be the first airmen in space. A clear and deliberate process. Without one, the odds are stacked even more against you, impossibly so.

Does your team need to be like the Rangers? Let's hope not, and that they're never called upon to do what the Rangers have to do. Does your team need to share a culture and a sense of identity? You'd better hope so, or your odds of success have just lengthened badly.

WHEN TO LEAD, WHEN TO FOLLOW, WHEN TO COLLABORATE

All positive efforts can come unstuck when a developing leader is unsure when to make a leader's call, and when to be just one of the team. With Flex, both leaders and followers have a clear understanding of their roles through each stage of the engine's cycle, and can help each other make the right calls.

In the planning stage, there is full engagement and collaboration. Through the agreed and defined process, all points of view are equally considered and respected. A draft course of action is worked through collaboratively, and only if there is a disagreement does the leader exercise a 51 percent vote to make a call and keep things moving. This is the beginning of the modern 'flat' organization. However, as we'll see, it's not the end.

When the team next gets together, it's for the brief. This is the leader's time. It is the only one-way communication in the Flex cycle. The leader has melded all of the team's input and situational awareness and is saying: 'Thanks for all the input, this is now the plan.' The team understands this and goes with the plan. It's not the time to challenge the leader.

Through the execution phase, the leader is just another member of the team with a defined role to play. People know what they have to do and are not looking to the leader for permission or direction. They are supported by wingmen, one of whom will be the leader.

When it's all over and the team regathers for the debrief, it's participation and collaboration again, with the leader having a special role to set the tone.

We'll push deeper into these phases very shortly, and see how Flex thinking offers the balances needed to bring the most out of the Flex processes, and the Flex teams.

PART B

THE FLEX ENGINE:
GETTING THINGS DONE

We're starting with the Flex engine because for most of us it is the most immediate place to start. Most of us know what our objectives are. We've been given them by our bosses, or worked them out with our colleagues. We are responsible, alone or with others, for getting our team there. If we need to start further back, with a High-definition (HD) Destination or a strategy to get there, we'll do that. But for now, let's assume we have a pretty good idea of where we're trying to go. The Flex engine is all about getting there, every time.

Up till now, we've tried to give you confidence that Flex works: that it can overcome complexity, it can keep ahead of the speed of change, and it can engage you and your team to be the best they can be. You know as well as we do the only thing that will give you that confidence is to try Flex. And to do this, you need a detailed account of how it works. That's what we're getting into now.

We have that confidence because we've used Flex so many times it is literally impossible to go about our days without using it, consciously and subconsciously. We have witnessed Flex save lives, including our own, too many times to think about. We have used it on leaving the air force to set up and run some very successful businesses, watched many fellow pilots do the same, and helped many more businesses become Flex businesses.

Here again is the Flex engine (see Figure 9). At this level, it's as simple as it looks. Plan–Brief–Execute–Debrief. Don't let that fool you. Each of its four steps is designed to stay on a path, wherever the path is heading and whatever obstacles are put in the way. The steps are simple in the sense that walking is simple: one-step-after-another simple, easy to see what's going on. But walking involves all the body's 206 bones and connecting tissue in ways too subtle to describe. There's a lot going on in those four steps! Remember, we were all a little wobbly the first time we took them.

Figure 9: Flex engine

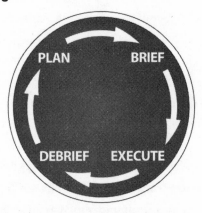

- **Plan.** The team deciding *who* does *what* by *when*, and *why* and *what-if*.
- **Brief.** A direct, personal, and concise communication of the plan by the leader, that calls the team and each individual from thought to action.
- **Execute.** The team working through its planned course of action, adjusting it as needed, with collective responsibility and individual accountability.
- **Debrief.** A blameless review of what happened, win or lose, and what can be learned to pivot to a new plan and action.

OK, let's get into it.

FLEX PLANNING

Fighter pilots hate surprises. It's hard enough hanging onto a jet at 700 miles per hour and 9 G. It's enough to fly formation, work the radar, listen to calls and monitor the dials and displays. It's harder still in combat, when tracking multiple targets, being locked onto by enemy craft, or dodging a surface-to-air missile. The last thing you need is something to come out of nowhere, something you really have to think about or you've lost your ass. There is no time to think. The time for thinking is on the ground.

Yet surprises do happen, and they can be nasty. Or, on the positive side, we might see the opportunity to pack a little bit more into a mission, to help out a unit on the ground, or take out a target that's come into view. We need the headspace to think when our operating environment changes. So the mission plan needs to be simple enough for us to take it all in at the briefing, but dynamic enough for us to respond when we need to.

That's why we plan missions *thoroughly*. It's not enough to know what to do, all going well, or even what to do if something goes wrong. We have to plan for every threat, for every contingency that any one of the planning team can think of. We want to minimize the things that can take us by surprise. That way we can respond as planned to things that pop up, and have the headspace to think if something completely unexpected happens.

Does that sound like your latest project, negotiation, or presentation? Well done if it does, truly. You know what it takes to get there. But for most of us in business, it sounds unrealistic. If we did that much thinking, we'd never get anywhere, right?

But Flex companies do. What we've described above gives the impression that planning occurs in isolation. In reality, it is part of a cycle. You've just completed a similar mission, and you've debriefed on what worked and what didn't. Yes, you have to plan for every contingency, but you've done the same thing last cycle. You know what is likely to happen. This becomes standard practice. You have to assume your team knows their standard practice. Remember: standards are your wings. You can't fly without them.

In fact, the secret of Flex planning is the way it balances three seemingly opposed sets of things. The Flex planning process is fast, yet considered—so that you have an effective plan when you need it. The resulting Flex plan is simple, yet dynamic—so that it nails the objective, changing as it needs to. And for those executing the plan, it is direct, yet empowering—so that they have clear accountability while being allowed the leeway to take the initiative they need.

Planning is the first stage in the Flex cycle, and it sets both the tone and the direction for the rest of the cycle. You brief the plan, the mission is the brief, and you debrief against the plan. So we're spending a little more time on understanding how the Flex way of thinking is harnessed at the planning stage, because that will flow through the rest of your performance.

FLEX PLANNING—FAST, YET CONSIDERED

One of our colleagues, 'Thor', embarked on an Executive MBA program soon after retiring from the air force in 2014. It was an intimidating class, full of bright young sparks and experienced hands, both looking to finesse their management skills. As in all such programs, teams had to work together in game-playing assignments, looking to outmaneuver other 'companies' from the same class in a hypothetical market. Thor was deeply impressed by his classmates' level of analysis and their ability to articulate it. They could out-think Sherlock and sell ice to an Eskimo, no doubt about it. So they laid out their points of view, and got ready to make their play. And ready. And ready. They got so close! Just a little more analysis. Ready, aim, aim, aim . . . a little more discussion . . . aim, aim. But they just couldn't get ready enough to say 'Fire!'

For Thor, this was a real eye-opener on the reality of organizational decision-making. People had the data, had the analysis, but didn't move. Even in the friendly, hypothetical market of the MBA classroom, hackles were rising. Opportunities passed by. Other teams got ahead. As the classmate with the least experience in corporate decisions, as much as he wanted to, Thor didn't feel he could push his team over the line. Finally though he could hold back no longer. He asked the team if they'd heard of a bias to action: the idea that inaction itself is a decision, and most often not the right one. The idea that by taking action new opportunities come up, new questions to answer, new things to practice. As long as the action wasn't fatal and was pointing in the right direction, go for it!

Blank faces among classmates is not a pleasant experience. No one was offended, but they took it courteously as an interesting perspective to add to their analysis, to which they returned. Just as Thor sank back into his chair, defeated, he noticed someone smiling across the circle. One of the class was an ex-Navy SEAL—who was thinking the same thing and had finally found a soulmate. A room full of ponderers was no match for two people with a bias to action. Together, they got things moving.

If taken sensibly, this bias to action is the antidote to paralysis by analysis. It is a bias much needed in fields of technology, for example, that hire graduates well versed in accessing, manipulating, and analyzing data, but less so in making the decisions on which that data is based. And that's a large proportion of the highly skilled, educated workforce we rely on.

By bias to action, we don't mean an urgency to crash through or crash. We mean an appreciation that the mission is upon us, that planning time is finite, that clear decisions are needed. Teams can't just go on and on about things. We are not building a consensus or taking a majority vote. The team leader has to make a timely call.

So, how can Flex planning be fast, yet still consider everything it needs to for an effective plan? To keep things moving, Flex relies on:

- **A known, shared, time-limited process.** This is for both our strategy and mission planning. Everyone knows the steps and what each step is aiming to reveal, and so each discussion is focussed and works through what it needs to in the time available.
- **Bias to action, acknowledging dynamic plans.** A Flex plan assumes that action needs to be taken sooner rather than later, and that the team itself will be making some decisions once that action starts. Bed down what you can in your planning time, then trust the skills, situational awareness, and initiative of your team.

This combination reduces the time you spend on your planning, so that it doesn't start to cut off options to act.

Fully considered

Flex planning needs to be fast, but your Flex plan still needs to be considered and effective. Four elements will help make sure it is: the right people taking part in open planning, taking part in a clear six-step process, focussed on the effects of the actions, and being independently reviewed by a Red Team as follows:

- **Open planning** means that all the right people are taking part in the planning: the people responsible for executing the plan, a more senior 'champion' who can resolve resource and conflict issues for them, and situation experts or specialists. Open planning, as in whole team planning, or 'teamstorming' as we call it, is one of the disciplined collaborations that makes Flex work. Every person who is part of the mission is part of the planning. If you need more specialists, bring them in. The more diverse the group, and the more perspectives, the better. Fighter pilots don't plan on their own, they bring in specialists from intelligence, maintenance, weather, weapons, and terrain who can contribute to 'building the picture' or have the situational awareness they need. Importantly in business, if the plan includes how you deliver what your client wants, think about including your client in the planning! Nothing beats that for improving the quality of both the plan and the client relationship. That's how we deal with complexity—build understanding across departments, and engage people from different generations.
- **Six-step planning process.** This same set, time-limited process is rigorous, so that all contributions are captured in an orderly way that leads to a clear course of action. The process starts with identifying the team's objective, and ends with a watertight plan for how to achieve it. It considers threats, available resources, and lessons learned. It lays out a clear course of action, ready to be briefed, and an execution cycle for keeping on track. We'll go through this process in depth in Chapter 6, 'Flex Planning'.

- **Effects-based planning** means that the planning and action will meet the leader's intent: a resulting effect that will take the team and its organization one step closer to its intended destination. The leader has to decide that intent *before* asking the team to plan the mission, so that the mission objective is sure to pursue that intent. It's an essential preliminary step in our planning process.
- **A Red Team review** is the last stage of our planning process. The Red Team review means that the whole plan gets stress-tested by a totally fresh set of experienced eyes. If a key specialist cannot be included in the planning team, make sure they're in the Red Team.

Flex planning works in good time because its processes offer a tight balance between speed and deliberation (see Table 1). They really tighten the gap between 'close enough is good enough' and 100 percent certainty. But you still need to make a call that you're ready to act. That call is the leader's judgment.

Table 1: Flex planning is . . .

Fast　　　　　　　　　yet . . .	Considered
• Time-limited process	• Open planning with all the right people
• Shared planning approach	• Effects-based planning
• Bias to action and dynamic plans	• Thorough six-step process + Red Team review
Balanced by . . . *Leader's Call*	

Apollo 13: A two-minute planning lesson

Not everyone is able to sit in on a military planning session. If you don't get that chance, have another look at the scene from the movie *Apollo 13* known as 'A New Mission' (just search that on YouTube). It happens pretty quickly, but it's all there. Shortly after Tom Hanks beams in with 'Houston, we have a problem', all the flight engineers at Mission Control are brought together. Ed Harris as mission commander Gene Kranz switches to 'failure is not an option' mode. He needs everyone there: it's open planning.

'OK people, listen up! I want you all to forget the flight plan. From this moment on, we are improvising a new mission.' The objective is to get the astronauts home. The threats are many and obvious. They identify the only engine capable of keeping the spacecraft going, and revisit what they know about it. Ideas are tossed up and thrown aside, and it starts looking impossible. The urgency adds pressure and makes it look more impossible.

Kranz ignores the fuss, and the overhead projector that inevitably doesn't work. He makes the call on the course of action—a slingshot around the moon. (That, incidentally, is classic problem solving: we have three options, two won't work, so we're taking the only one with half a chance.) The engineers start work on sub-plans to meet the many threats, among them that the capsule will run out of power well before reaching earth.

FLEX PLANS—SIMPLE, YET DYNAMIC

The more complex a plan, the more likely it will fail. The more steps it has, the more detailed the instruction, the greater the chance of human error. A simple plan means that the people accountable for it are absolutely clear on *who* does *what* and *when.* There can be no ambiguity around those three steps. So that's a plan, right? *Who* does *what* and *when.* That's what most of us think of as a plan, and what common templates to lay out an action plan allow room for.

Flex calls for a little more, and that little more makes all the difference. We can put it in the same simple terms:

A Flex plan answers *who, what, when* . . . and *why* and *what-if.*

These two additional little questions carry a lot of weight.

Answering *why?* means not only confirming the mission's immediate objective, but also why it has that objective. We will talk about the mission's alignment with your organizational strategy and your team leader's intent in Part C, 'The Flex cockpit and wings'. For now, it's worth bearing in mind that any mission plan needs to take into account three potential outcomes: its primary operational objective, the effect the mission will have on relationships with people that matter, and the effect it will have on the learning and culture of your own team. We need to remember the differences between business and the military. Any business effort is primarily a social effort: for it to succeed, we have to decide how best to work with the people involved in that effort.

Answering *what-if?* makes sure that you've thought of the threats, the things you can't control that have a greater or lesser chance of happening. These include, of course, the threats to that social effort: the reactions and resistances of the people involved. But keeping the 'what-if' separate achieves an extremely important outcome: focus. So often in our planning workshops, we see teams argue about 'what-if', so that the first task of any possible plan wilts on the vine before seeing the light of day. Yet the world *is* an imperfect place, and we need to test our plan against the things that *may* go wrong. As they say in the squadrons: 'Plan for perfection, prepare for the worst.'

These two questions—*why?* and *what-if?*—are what makes your plan dynamic, able to respond to changing conditions and realities as you execute the mission. It engages people to achieve their mission, and makes the plan both threat- and time-sensitive. If a team has situational awareness, and knows why they're on the mission, they can adjust their plan so that it still delivers what's needed, if at all possible. And if it's not possible, they can abort the plan. All this is essential if your operating environment is in any way complex or unpredictable. A Flex plan calls on your team to be engaged on their mission, not robotic.

It's just as important to recognize one question that's missing: *how*. That seems counter-intuitive, right? Isn't a plan just that— how to get something done? That's right. But by answering those five little questions, we've answered the *how* for that mission.

The Flex plan sets out what each person on the team needs to do. If it tries to answer *how* they're going to do that, it's at the wrong level. That's for the individual team member to answer, or the next team down. If your plan sets out how something in the plan is to be done, then it's pretending it's an instruction to a machine, and forgetting it's a plan for a team. If you never need to engage people, if you never need them to react to a change in circumstances, then don't plan the mission—just write out your step-by-step procedures and get your robots to follow them. But if you try that with people, don't expect them to follow your lead for long.

There is a distinction to make here. When we get to executing the plan, you will want to draw on checklists and standards—fixed routines that you know work, that calm you for action, and that free up your mind to make decisions that matter. They may be the company standards or procedures that have to be followed. They may be your own techniques that you've developed and trust, and that your team respects. But these are *not* part of the plan—they're your wings, what you rely on when you're in action.

Balancing simple and dynamic: the execution rhythm

As with the planning process itself, a Flex plan must be in balance. It must be simple enough for there to be no confusion as to *who* does *what* and *when*. Yet it must also be dynamic, so that each *what-if* event has a response, and each opportunity can be considered.

At some point in the planning process, as the contingencies and the variables mount up, the plan will start to lose its clarity. There are too many *what-ifs*, too many options for people to take, too many possibilities that may change the game.

How can a Flex team keep that balance? By setting what we call the 'execution rhythm' for that strategy or mission. Every mission and strategy has an execution rhythm (see Table 2). The rhythm is the timespan after which the team needs to check in that it's on target and that the plan is working. For shorter missions, that may be the end of each day or the end of the mission. For a fighter squadron, a mission is always less than a day. In business, it could be anything from an hour's trading or conference session, to a week's sales cycle.

For a mission that's any longer than a week, you're going to have to set an execution rhythm as part of the plan. When will it make sense for the team to come back in and review their progress against the mission objective, or to start on a new plan for a new mission objective? A plan should not try to lay out its course too far into the future. There are too many unknowns. A strategy can look into the distance, knowing that a host of mission plans are needed for the strategy to be fulfilled. But each mission plan must keep its execution rhythm tight. We explore more about the execution rhythm in Chapter 9, 'Execute (keeping people to the plan)'.

Table 2: A Flex plan is . . .

Simple and Direct yet . . .	Dynamic and Empowering
• Clear, measurable, achievable, objective	• *Why* allows for initiative, for taking opportunities with situational awareness and alignment
• Clear course of action: *who* does *what* and *when?*	• *What-if* covers contingencies
• Able to briefed, personally and precisely	• Relies on team standards and individual techniques (avoids *How*)
Balanced by . . . Execution Rhythm	

FLEX PLANS—DIRECT, YET EMPOWERING

There is no waffle in a Flex plan. The whole point of it is for people to know exactly *what* they need to achieve by *when*, for every task in the plan. In that sense every task is stated as its own mission objective, and the same rules apply: it must be clear, measurable, and achievable. And so it will become part of a Flex brief: direct, personal, and concise. So how does any of that empower anyone?

We cannot emphasize two characteristics of Flex planning enough. People are working out *their own* plans, and those plans do not include *how* to do things. These two characteristics have long been consistent with better motivation and performance at work. In the 1980s, several studies showed that people worked harder, were more satisfied, and trusted their employers more if their management supported their autonomy: respecting perspectives, giving choices, and encouraging self-initiation rather than specifying how they should do things.[1] For the millennial generation, support for autonomy is even more important. Millennials will be more energized and productive if they have greater autonomy over where, when, and how they work.[2]

Again, there is a balance to be reached between the directness of a Flex plan, and the need for team members to have control of their own missions. That balance is found in the team's situational awareness (see Chapter 12, 'Situational awareness'). The more awareness the team has of the context for the mission, the state of the industry, its players and history, the less direction they will need.

The team's own plans

Flex plans are created by the teams who are responsible for executing them. In being part of their team, in taking part in their planning, people are signing up to the team's plan. They are making commitments to their team, and the Flex experience is that those commitments will hold.

In *The Upside of Turbulence,* another book that helps leadership deal with complex times, MIT Professor Donald Sull suggests that 'The best promises share five characteristics: they are public, active, voluntary, explicit, and they include a clear rationale for why they matter.'[3] Each of these characteristics is shared by the commitments made in Flex planning. When a team works together to set its mission plan for a worthwhile, aligned objective, the team members have no problem buying in to the plan or being responsible to take on the needed tasks. If anything, the team needs to watch for people who overload themselves with tasks. But as we'll see in Chapter 9, 'Execute (keeping people to the plan)', there are ways to manage that risk.

Only include what's needed

A Flex plan does not go into the detail of *how* its tasks are to be done, nor state the obvious, nor restate standards. Just like the strategy it is pursuing, the mission is defined only by its intended effect: the *what*. Similarly, each task in the mission plan is defined only by its intended effect: *what* by *when* by *who*; clear, measurable, achievable. How that result occurs is up to the team (for the mission) or the individual (for the task).

The classic story to distinguish the *what* from the *how* comes from the 1898 Spanish–American War, when the U.S. intervened in the Cuban War of Independence.[4] The story goes that President McKinley wanted to get a message to a commander of the Cuban rebels, Calixto Garcia. The mission was given to lieutenant Andrew Rowan, with no more detail than 'Get this message to Garcia'—no one knew where Garcia was, what he looked like, or how to contact him. But that was the president's intent, and was all Rowan needed. Six weeks and enough adventure to fill two movies and a radio play later, the message was delivered. The phrase 'Take a message to Garcia' is still used in the military to say to a team: 'You work it out.' That's all a good team wants to hear.

So if your plan calls for Tom to have a car outside 1135 North Street at 11 p.m., it's Tom's task to get it there. You don't want to get into the route taken, the speed driven, the need to obey traffic laws, the need for fuel. You don't want to worry about the way Tom drives. Your team will have standard operating procedures (SOPs). It's obvious the car needs gas in the tank and air in the tires. These are 'breathing' steps: steps so obvious it's like telling people to remember to breathe. Beyond that, leave it to Tom to drive the car his way, using whatever techniques and preferences he likes—and that are consistent with the SOPs. If you go into too much detail, if you belabor the obvious, it's an insult to people. They're on the team to do these things—let them work it out, or ask for support.

As Charles Duhigg said in *The Power of Habit*: 'Giving employees a sense of agency—a feeling that they are in control, that they have a genuine decision-making authority—can radically increase how much energy and focus they bring to their jobs.'[5] Or, remember how General Patton put it: 'Don't tell people how to do things. Tell them what to do, and let them surprise you with the results.'

NOT YOUR TYPICAL PLAN

Some of what we say about Flex planning in this and the next chapter will be familiar to you from your own experience. But we would be very surprised if the whole process is familiar, more so if it is a process you're following now. Here are some of the differences we find when talking about planning with our clients, which are summarised in Table 3.

For starters, most planning is done by people other than the team that is going to execute it. The more complex the task, the wider that gap becomes. There are planning and project management specialists who are tasked with degree-demanding software to work out 'the plan'. There are strategy teams who sit apart from operating divisions to work out 'the plan'. Even in small groups, team leaders work long into the night to figure out exactly how their team will work, without including their teams in the plan. Flex planning ensures a realistic course of action, because the people setting the course are the people (or their teams) who will be running it.

Second, most planning starts by looking back: by rolling out the plan from last time. If it worked, it can be repeated, no? By rolling out the last plan, you're also rolling out all its assumptions about the context, threats, and resources available. It may or may not work, but it will never get better. Instead, Flex planning starts with the future: it looks forward to the mission objective. With that single peg holding down a clean sheet, the team can look without distraction at what they have to do, what they have to help them, and what may stop them.

The next most obvious difference is the amount of analysis that goes into Flex planning. If you're updating the last plan, and then handing it to the 'doers', there isn't really that much consideration of new data and current affairs. Mostly, there is a list of tasks that is updated and lengthened. Sometimes, the

Table 3: Flex planning
The planning process . . .

Flex	Traditional
• Is led by the operational team	• Is led by the planning team
• Involves the whole business	• Involves a silo or project team
• Starts with objectives	• Starts with last time
• Focusses on tasks and effects	• Focusses on analysis
• Deals with threats in course of action	• Deals with threats in separate risk management plan

The resulting plan is . . .

Flex	Traditional
• Simple	• Requires project management software
• Fresh	• A replay of yesterday
• Flexible	• Set
• Action-orientated	• Conceptual

reason why a task is on the list has been forgotten, but no one is brave enough to remove it for fear of unknown consequences. Flex teams know the purpose of each step in the course of action, because they've put it there to get one step closer to the mission objective, or to address a threat.

Which is where we deal with threats—in the plan. Most plans set out a solid string of actions, and then have a section called 'risk management'. These are additional steps that are likely to be needed, but are held apart from the main flow. In Flex planning, if a material threat can be controlled in any way, that control is part of the course of action. That way, we know the course of action works as a whole with or without those threats. If the threat is uncontrollable, then a contingency plan will come into operation at a decision point with a known trigger. There are no floating risks left as part of a risk management plan that may never be reviewed until it's needed, when a review is too late.

Finally, and we'll talk about this through the next two chapters, Flex planning only stops when the mission stops. It is continuously adapting to realities, which the team leader continually reviews. It continues through to the moment of the brief, pauses only to start the mission, and then continues right through it.

7

THE SIX-STEP MISSION PLANNING PROCESS

A good Flex engine has a continuous cycle, and you may find yourself picking up this book at any one of its four stages. But we're starting with mission planning because it lays the foundation and the terminology for the other three stages. As we've seen in the previous chapters, Flex planning is a relatively fast yet considered process. What the team needs to achieve is set by its leader, but the planning itself is done by the whole team, with any outsider subject experts or facilitators you feel would add insight. It needs that diversity of thinking to make sure that the plan is as solid as possible. And it needs the people who are about to execute the mission. For the purpose of planning, they know what they can and can't do, how they will do it, and what they will need. And when it comes to the mission itself, they will own it.

A Flex plan starts with what the team leader intends the mission to achieve—the *why*—and finishes with the team's clearer mission objective and the course of action to get there. Together, the 'leader's intent' and the course of action will answer the *who, what, when* . . . and *why* and *what-if*. Throughout the military and business there are variations on these six steps, but our experience suggests the following steps will get you where you need to go.

1. Set a **mission objective**, meeting the leader's intent, that is clear, measurable, and achievable. (Where do we need to be, and why?)
2. Identify any **threats**, controllable and not. (What's in the way?)
3. Identify the **resources** you can draw on. (What can help us to our objective, or deal with what's in the way?)
4. Identify the **lessons learned** from previous debriefs that you can draw on.
5. Set out a **course of action**: *who* does *what* and *when* to reach the objective?
6. Set your **contingency** plans, the *what-ifs*. Prepare for the worst.

OK, looks like a plan? Not yet. Get the Red Team to find holes in the plan, and plug them.

THE LEADER'S INTENT

No matter how clearly defined your achievable objective is, there has to be a point to it: to get your team and your organization one step closer to your ultimate destination. That gives the mission purpose, and that purpose motivates your team. There's a point to the mission, and the team knows it. It's up to the team leader to make that purpose clear. The mission planning will set a specific, immediate objective, but the leader's intent is the intended effect of that mission. That is the intent that the leader owns. As we've seen, the team itself will take ownership for the objective and the plan to meet it.

All of this is about aligning your team's mission towards your high-definition vision of your destination (HD Destination). Each mission is planned to pursue a strategy or campaign towards the HD Destination. It may go exactly as planned, it may go a little off course, or it may be opportunistic—but every mission is pointing in the right direction. Without that clear alignment, good people are on good missions that may seem worthwhile, but don't advance the team or the organization towards its goals. In a world with infinite time and resources, that may be OK, but not in the world we know and love.

One of our colleagues, a special forces operator, left the military after a distinguished ten-year career and began managing a 50-person sales force for a medical company. They were a terrific team. Their numbers were outstanding, sales were up, particularly in smaller markets. Doctors in rural hospitals loved the company's product and were often able to buy it without involving a larger bureaucracy, so that's where many salespeople focussed. What was not to like?

Turns out, plenty. The company had a problem aligning its sales teams with its corporate goals, and management was not happy. The company wanted to build their products' reputation by having them used by the best physicians in the finest hospitals, by prestigious institutions like the Mayo Clinic and Johns Hopkins. Instead, they were being sold into rural hospitals with little influence elsewhere. The salesforce were growing sales, but not in the way that would help the company's ultimate goals. They met their mission objectives, but the objective wasn't aligned with the company's purpose. The intent of the sales team leader was misdirected, or not clearly stated to the team.

Going back 70 years, it's worth retelling two air stories from World War II to really press home this idea of alignment.

No prizes for guessing the overall objective of the Allied forces in World War II—to win the war in Europe. Their strategy against the enemy included three critical leverage points: breaking the will of the German people, attacking the German military and industrial complex, and maintaining the Allies' own supply lines. That strategy demanded any number of missions to be completed, and the effort accelerated in the lead up to the D-Day landing of 156,000 Allied forces on the beaches of northern France to take mainland Europe back from fascism.

In the one-year lead up to D-Day, the question for Allied military planners was how to weaken the German war machine before the D-Day troops landed. An unknown star at an unknown planning session identified that pretty much every machine in the Nazi war effort relied on one single, simple product—ball bearings. Tanks, planes, trucks, trains, you name it, if it was big and it moved, it needed bearings. And most of the ball bearings were made in a single German town, Schweinfurt. On Allied military maps, those factories earned themselves a big red target cross.

The Schweinfurt factories were bombed on 17 August 1943. It was a double-strike mission—the other target being Messerschmitt aircraft factories in nearby Regensburg—with a strike force of 376 bombers and 459 fighter escorts. The novel and film *Twelve O'Clock High* reasonably captures the intent and execution of these missions. The 60 aircraft lost on the night was more than double the previous biggest Allied loss in a single mission. Was it worth it? Destroying the Regensburg factories meant a 34 percent drop in Messerschmitt production, a tremendous effect from the Allied perspective. But the Schweinfurt mission brought less joy.

Remarkably, the bombers hit their targets. At night and without 21st-century laser guidance, they reached, sighted, and bombed the factories—80 direct hits—and visually confirmed damage to 1.4 million square feet (130,000 square meters) of buildings. Despite the dreadful losses (more on that in a moment), the mission objective had been met.

The problem was that if your leader's intent was to remove

ball bearings from the German war diet, the factories weren't the real targets. The real targets were the machinery inside the factories that made the ball bearings, and the stores of ball bearings elsewhere. Neither were touched. The bombers did a great job of blowing holes in factory roofs and knocking down factory walls, but they didn't reach the machinery inside. After the raids, the Germans dusted off the machinery, put a tarp over them, brought in brickmasons, and got back to work making ball bearings. There were no follow-up raids. And, after the war, long-held stockpiles of ball bearings were found all over Germany. The mission objective had been met, but its *purpose* had not. The mission objective was poor: though clear, measurable, and (just) achievable, it was not closely enough aligned with the strategy, its effects not clearly enough planned.

The losses from the Schweinfurt–Regensburg mission were severe enough for the Allies to stop long-range bombing missions for five months. The causes of those losses were many, not least having no fighter support for almost two-thirds of their time in the air. Another reason for their losses may have been the role of the fighter jets that *did* escort the bombers in World War II. Our next story is another example of how a seemingly excellent mission objective may fail for its lack of alignment.

This story concerns the Tuskegee Airmen of the U.S. Air Force's 332nd Fighter Group. They were famed for three reasons: their P-51 Mustangs were painted with red tails (hence the movie *Red Tails*), they were African Americans (initially facing immense prejudice as the first in the USAF), and yet they were the fighter escorts of choice for U.S. bombers from late 1944.

Fighter escorts had the dangerous and critical task of protecting Allied bombers against German planes trying to shoot them down. You would think, then, that the escorts were rated and rewarded for escorting their bombers safely to and from their targets? Not so. Fighter pilots in the U.S. Army Air Forces (as they were known in

World War II) were rewarded for one thing only—shooting down enemy fighters. They could paint a swastika on their jet for every downed enemy, and if you shot down five jets, you were an 'Ace', with all the respect and privileges that status brought.

Knowing this, the German fighters would make themselves live bait. They'd try to engage with the Allied escorts and draw them away from the bombers and into a dogfight. That would leave the bombers protected only by their own guns, no real match for a second wave of Messerschmitts.

Of all the U.S. squadrons, only the Tuskegee decided, as a squadron, not to take the bait on escort missions. They made their mission the same as the bombing mission: getting to the drop zone and home again, safely. They lost bombers on only seven of 179 escort missions, about half the average of other fighter groups. They didn't really care about being Aces—they had plenty of combat missions to prove their mettle.

STEP 1: SET THE MISSION OBJECTIVE

It's hard to overstate the value of a good mission objective. People really like to know what they are trying to do, and why that's worth doing. That's why they've joined your team, your club, your business, your government. So if a good mission objective is given to them, you're off to a good start. But a Flex mission objective is one people help to create themselves, and that takes their motivation to a whole new level. The military might say 'Give me a mission objective well suited to my skills and in line with the leader's intent, and I'm willing to risk my life. That's what I'm trained to do.' A poor mission objective will leave your team, and you, cold.

This is true of both short-term and long-term missions. A short-term mission has the advantage of being something that you and I can go out and start executing *today*. If you don't have clarity around that, it will be a long day out. But a poor objective for a long-term mission, even an organizational strategy? We're wasting years, resources, careers. Don't do that. A Flex mission objective will be clear, measurable, achievable, and aligned.

Clear

Mission objectives should be CLEAR. That means that everyone briefed to do the job knows exactly what the objective is. The mission objective is a sentence, and you have to test two things about a sentence: the words and the order you put them in.

Push hard on the meaning of every word. If it's an acronym, does your team know what it stands for? If it's a generic business term (sales, competition, costs), have you given a precise definition? You don't want to be arguing about it after the event. If it's a technical term used in your company, does everyone in the team know exactly what it means? If there's any shadow of a doubt, you can be sure that someone on your team will interpret the word the wrong way. Someone will get hurt. Don't give them that chance.

Measurable

If you get the words and structure right, your objective will be clear and unambiguous. That idea slides into it being measurable. Immediately after the mission, you'll be asking 'Did we achieve our objective?' There are only two answers that matter—'yes' or 'no'. Everyone must be able to answer 'yes' or 'no'—as soon as the mission is complete. Anything else means you haven't framed a clear and measurable objective.

To be measurable, to be able to say 'yes' or 'no', means you've got a specific action or number and time in the objective that can be measured objectively. If there's a number involved, you need to be able to chart it. If there's a checklist involved, you need to be able to tick it off. If the mission is to 'launch a product', be clear on the measures that will determine whether the product has, in fact, been launched.

In the same vein, a mission objective must be to do something tangible, not to increase or improve a quality or characteristic, no matter how desirable. Don't ask a team to 'lift the quality of the pipe housing' or 'improve collaboration'. Quality and collaboration can be measured, but only if you set out clearly what that measure will be: 'Our company will develop a new product that will meet 10 percent of the forecast demand of our top four Asia-Pacific customers by 1 December 2017.' What have we achieved in that mission objective? In one sentence we have aligned R&D, logistics, marketing, sales, HR area managers and executives to what we are going to do and how we know whether we've done it.

Finally, a measure is an objective measure, not an opinion. Don't ask your team to go out there and bust a gut when the objective is 'to hold the event to Pete's satisfaction'. Would that be Pete in a good mood or a bad mood? At the event or elsewhere? Conscious or unconscious? Objectives and opinions don't mix. It's a lot more productive to get rid of the opinions.

Achievable

Mission objectives have to be achievable. Nothing erodes motivation and energy faster than being asked to do the impossible. Tough missions can be great challenges that bind a team forever. A mission can be a stretch, it can ask for a brutal effort. But it has to be possible.

All countries and too many movies have tales of heroic action by soldiers who have either attacked or defended impossible positions, inevitably at the cost of their own lives. For Australia and New Zealand, it's the assault on Lone Pine at ANZAC Cove in 1915. For the U.S. it's the Battle of the Bulge in 1944–45 and the taking of Iwo Jima in 1945. For the United Kingdom and Europe, it's Waterloo in 1815, the Somme in 1916, or Stalingrad in 1943. These are stories from another age. For the modern army and air force, the loss of one life means that a mission has failed. Leaders who ask for another's inevitable sacrifice—where an option exists— immediately lose their respect. Business is not life and death, but the concepts of sacrifice and respect are real enough. A team or an individual that's on a road to nowhere will not travel it far.

Fortunately, the Flex planning process will determine whether an objective is achievable or not, and the team itself is leading that process. If it looks impossible, there are options. The team may seek additional resources. More often, the objective can be adjusted. The best adjustment is to shorten the reach of the mission. If the original mission looks impossible yet still valuable, break it down into steps and make the first one achievable. Then see what's possible from there.

Mission testing

Let's look at some mission objectives and see if they pass our four tests.

Train the sales staff on the new product.

OK, too easy, not even close to clear.

Train all client-facing sales staff
on the capabilities and design of the new Dynamo 9000.

That's certainly clearer, but is it measurable? Yes, it is—we can tell whether training was conducted, and whether all relevant staff attended. Is that important? It could be, if our firm was having trouble setting up classroom training and getting people to come. But it's unlikely to be the effect we're looking for. More likely is for the sales staff to have the knowledge they need to talk to clients about the new product. That means introducing a different measure.

*Conduct classroom training on the new Dynamo 9000 so that
all client-facing sales staff know 90 percent or more of the
critical product information by 1 February 2016.*

Now we're getting somewhere. But is it where we want to be?
We can now see that the effect we're looking for is not completed
training, but sales staff knowledge. If that's the effect we're looking
for, do we need to direct the team on how to achieve that effect?
If this is a mission for the learning and development team, do
we need to say how they should get that information into the
heads of the sales staff? Not really—that's what the L&D team
will work out in their course of action. In the mission objective
above, we are thinking more narrowly than we need to. The
following mission objective would serve us better—it is direct,
yet empowering:

*Ensure that all client-facing sales staff know and can use
90 percent or more of the critical Dynamo 9000 product
information by 1 February 2016.*

And with the Dynamo 9000 being launched on 1 February,
we can be pretty confident that this mission will be aligned with
the firm's strategy.

STEP 2: IDENTIFY MISSION THREATS

As a fighter pilot, someone was out there wanting to shoot us
down. We wanted to know everything, but nothing, about who
those people were and what their jets could do. You get very
serious about gathering information when your life is on the line.

The threats may not be as deadly in business, but they are
just as real and just as threatening to your career and company.
'Be paranoid!' Intel's first CEO Andy Grove used to say. Paranoid

in the most constructive of ways. Dig down and really work out what your weaknesses are, what could go wrong, what could go so right that it would distract you from your actual objective, and also what your competition could do. There will be threats, no matter how seemingly straightforward a mission is.

At this stage of planning, your team needs to identify what your threats are—internal and external—and whether you can control them. Like everything in Flex and life, you're aiming at a sweet spot: not too few threats that you miss some, not too many that they become demoralizing and your plan to meet them becomes chaotic.

It's here too that it's worth making an effort to be able to classify your threats. This helps your team to discuss those threats, to work out how important they are, to work out what to do with them. If a threat is controllable you can plan for that control in your course of action. If it's not, you'll need a contingency plan.

Most of all though, make sure that you note *all* risks brought up in the planning session. Don't leave anything out until you've done the triage described in the section 'Threat triage', later in this chapter.

Internal threats

'We have met the enemy, and he is us.' So said Walt Kelly to introduce his *Pogo* cartoon in 1953, as with so many cartoonists so dangerously close to home truths. It's a great line, because it points you one way, then brings you back to the place that matters.[1]

We might try to deny it, but our personal, internal threats are the most common. We get distracted; we lose confidence, focus, energy, or the will to lead. These are ever-present threats that we deal with in the *execution* phase of the Flex cycle. There are systematic, effective actions to combat these threats, but it would serve no purpose building them into the team's course of action. (If they are particularly relevant to a mission or to one of the team, then the leader will mention them in the brief, in a pointer to a specific standard that will be relied on.)

The internal threats that we're most interested in here are those, relevant to the mission, which exist within your team or the organization itself. Do you have the resources and funding you need? Do you have the senior leadership support—really? Do you have the skilled personnel? There may be less obvious threats. Are there any relationships within the team that might blow up through the mission? Are your communication lines and methods as clear as they need to be? Will you have the information you need to make decisions when you need to?

We have been working with the pharmaceutical company Pfizer for many years, a company that has seen incredible scientific and market changes over those two decades. Long ago, we worked with the Australian sales and marketing team on their year's product plans. When we got to the threats, the room buzzed with what their competitors were going to do, the new products on the line, the tightening of government funding for prescription drugs. All the usual stuff. It took a while, but in the end they saw that the biggest threat was internal: a personality and priorities gulf between the medical and marketing teams. Sound familiar?

In the pharmaceutical industry, there are scientists who work on the next generation of drugs, medical specialists who conduct trials to secure their safe and approved use, and marketing teams who gather the best information to plan and launch promotions and direct sales teams. Medical guys are properly scientific, cautious, unwilling to make any product claims until all the evidence is in. Marketing and sales guys are outgoing, looking for action, itching to take great new products to their clients. The medical department wasn't supplying marketing with the trial outcomes, or even the trial timelines. They weren't stonewalling, they just had fundamental legal obligations to fulfill, against which marketing timelines weren't considered important.

That was a while ago, and now the departments at Pfizer each appreciate the others' roles and obligations more clearly. In no small part, that was due to their working on their annual product plans together. Everyone in the building wanted good new Pfizer products being prescribed by their clients. Once they talked together through the process and demands of getting them to market, the plans for doing so were in much better shape.

The biggest internal threat we see across all our clients? We call it CIA. Not trying to be funny or disrespectful, these are the deadly triad of *complacency, indifference, and apathy*. They can appear anywhere: in you, in your team, your customers, your boss. People who just possibly don't care about your mission anywhere as much as you need them to. With CIA, your team is not really going to consider its threats. You've assumed them away. Nothing to worry about here. And so have the rest of your organization: they've got their own issues to deal with, so don't expect them to save you from yourself. Hey, some of them might even want to see you crash and burn! Back to Andy Grove—be paranoid. Use Flex and you won't have to deal with CIA. We prepare for the worst and you'll enjoy your best.

External threats

Again, you need to be as curious and imaginative as possible to identify threats to your mission that come from outside your organization. They will depend on the nature of your mission and its timeframe. For example, if your mission is a one-day event, you'll need to consider anything that could disrupt it: the weather, your IT connectivity, other public and private events in the vicinity, delivery access, roadworks, the withdrawal of key guests, loss of power. If you're holding your event at a large hotel or convention center, you're paying others to eliminate many of those threats, but not all. If you're in charge of an outside location, then it will be up to your team. If you're giving a speech or presentation, you might want to consider whether anything would make the content matter redundant, or worse. A comedian tells the sorry story of telling a string of great gags about a divisive public figure, only to be met by stony and horrified faces. Did he know the figure had died overnight? Should he have checked? Should he have had other material? Make up a checklist of the world of possible threats—weather, logistics, audience, content—and run through it as a habit.

For more significant business missions, the external threats are larger, but are unlikely to emerge without warning. For these, you may well need a framework to act as your team's checklist. The business of CTG Global was to get people into dangerous situations, keep them healthy, and get them out again. That was the checklist of threats for Boo and Tom: In–Alive–Out. There was no travel agent capable of getting their people safely to the worksite, overcoming disputed visas or transport interruptions, and either corrupt, overzealous, or overly suspicious officials. To keep their people safe, they paid over the odds in wages, security, and insurances; maintained a fleet of specially secured vehicles; and spent most of their time building and keeping relationships. All this was happening in a cash economy, so securing cash became a daily mission of its own.

Yet the biggest threat to CTG's business was the loss of its reputation. If it could not look after its employees, the best Gurkha families would no longer work with them. If those workers could not do the job they were assigned, the UN and Western firms would no longer contract with CTG Global. So every CTG assignment started with a two-week no-questions-asked probation period. If the client wasn't happy with the worker, or the worker wasn't happy with the client, the worker would come home. No other personnel firm in the Middle East operated that way, and no other firm grew as fast or as surely.

In more familiar business environments, the threats may be

more obvious, but equally dangerous to your business. Clear sources of threats are your competitors' actions and miscommunicating with your business partners. You can't expect your own business partners to think and act the way you do. Some partners will have similar ways of communicating to you, others won't. Some will make their displeasures known face-to-face, others will smile congenially at a meeting but make an unexpected decision. They're not being dishonest, they may simply come from cultures where confrontation is avoided. It's up to you to find out where they really stand, in private conversations between trusted partners. These realities, and how your team communicates through them, are threats that lie in wait for any business and personal dealing with someone from another 'crowd', whether the crowd is across town or across an ocean.

Think also of the triple bottom line of profit, people, and planet. What is happening in your market: your competitors; economic, regulatory, and technology trends? What social and environmental shifts are occurring that may change assumptions about the resources you have available? Have your competitors been quiet for a while, but still securing capital? Will water be available in the quality and quantity you need? Are people more comfortable with online transactions, even with strangers in peer-to-peer models, making old brands more susceptible? Are peer-to-peer models gearing up for the same regulation that traditional hire and lease businesses face? Will a new transport hub make your old central location an old and dustier option? Will your customers still be happy to pay you in cash, when they really like paying online and tracking their expenses through apps? Is the price of gas rising faster than interest rates are falling?

Keep building your knowledge on trends that will affect your business, in any respect. Any one of them might decide to announce itself on your mission. Keep building up your potential responses. Use each mission planning episode as an opportunity to quickly check in on those trends. It's standard risk analysis. Are any of those risks becoming real? Are any ready to manifest themselves?

While those longer trends build and bubble in the background, the news of the week may bring any one of them sharply into focus. Let's say you're planning a new brand or product launch, with a tagline something safely generic, like 'direct action'. Imagine that two days before the launch, a political party launches a new policy initiative called 'Direct Action'. Their policy is a million miles from your business initiative; their action has nothing to do with yours. But the political policy has been widely panned in the media, for reasons again nothing to do with your business. Do you go ahead? Maybe, maybe not. But if you're not aware of what's happening, whatever choice you make will likely be the wrong one.

This is what we mean by situational awareness, the need to understand your operating environment and what's happening in it (see Chapter 12, 'Situational awareness'). It's also an example of what our colleague Serge would call the threat of 'losing control of the message'. You never know who's going to come out with a message that is potentially damaging to your mission—one of your own team, or any third party. Though you can try to control that message, you can never do so completely, so the test will be how you react to it.

Controllable or uncontrollable threats

Controllable means that the planning team can negate, mitigate, or avoid the threat. That is, the team can take some action so that the threat does not take place (negate it) or, if it does, it will not affect the mission because its impact is reduced (mitigated), or the mission is planned so that it doesn't matter if the threat is realized or not (avoided). If the team can control a material threat, it should do so in its course of action—the plan includes an action to control the threat (Step 4). If the team can't control the threat, it becomes a contingency (Step 6)—the plan will change if the event occurs.

It's not always easy to distinguish between controllable and uncontrollable threats. Let's take the perennially safe ground of the weather. You've got an outdoor event coming up, and it may rain. You can control that threat—either by mitigating it (umbrellas and sturdy marquees) or avoiding it (holding it indoors). But a thunderstorm? If you've gone ahead with the outdoor event, a crashing storm is pretty much uncontrollable. You'll need a contingency plan, and a time to decide whether to put that plan into action.

Threats to a business mission can be just as uncontrollable. Most of us are price takers in our markets. We can hedge some of those prices—gas, interest rates, currency, commodities—over certain timeframes, but not all prices for all times. Property developers find themselves exposed when interest rates rise or employment falls just enough to trigger a downturn in prices, or approval delays push their build times out to the peak of the market, leaving them to sell on the downslope. You may be able to mitigate risks in an approval process, but perfectly pick the swings in the market? What's the contingency plan when that threat materializes?

Threat triage

Your team will have identified any number of threats, large and small, likely and unlikely, controllable and uncontrollable. Now it has to decide what to do with them. Remember that we're not talking long-term strategy here, but planning a specific, short-term mission. We can control the variables. If it's a longer-term mission, we'll have a chance to change the plan.

First, analyze the risks with two questions: what impact would the threats have on the mission, and what is their likelihood of occurring? Use a loose scale—low–medium–high is fine—and let your team discuss and vote on them.

In assessing the impact of the risks, you may want to consider the categories of risk Jim Collins used in *Great by Choice* as summarised in Figure 10.[2] Every mission worth taking will have risks. The ones you want to be really careful of are as follows:

- **Death line risks**, which would seriously damage your team or organization. Don't bet the house. No surprises there.
- **Asymmetric risks**, in which the downside is considerably greater than the mission's upside. This is a great reminder to compare the upside and downside. Don't risk your wall to put up a nice painting.
- **Uncontrollable risks** that expose the team or organization to forces or events that it cannot control. Again, a nice way of thinking of things. Think twice before you unleash what you don't understand and can't control. If you are going to wake up a sleeping competitor, you better be sure it's worth it, and that you can control the response.

When you think about it, all of these risks are asymmetric: they are not worth taking, whatever may be gained by the mission. There is really only one question when it comes to risks or threats: is achieving the objective worth the possible price (in whatever form) that may have to be paid? If the answer is 'yes', then the mission should proceed and the threats, hazards, or risks should be accepted and, if possible, mitigated. If the risks are serious and probable enough, then the mission will need to be put aside. The team will have to set a less risky immediate objective that puts it in a safer place to reach the ultimate objective.

Second, determine whether the threats are controllable or uncontrollable. If controllable, the controlling action will be in your course of action. They will each be mitigated or avoided as part of your plan. If the threats are uncontrollable, you'll need a contingency plan . . . a *what-if*.

The lower priority threats are not forgotten. The fact that you've taken this step in your planning means your team is aware of these threats. If they arise, you'll be in a much better position to respond to them appropriately. You will have situational awareness—both about the threats, and about the mission situation. There may be a simple response, or the team might quickly review ideas. Either way, you won't have been taken by surprise, and you won't overreact in a way that may jeopardise the mission.

Figure 10: Threat triage

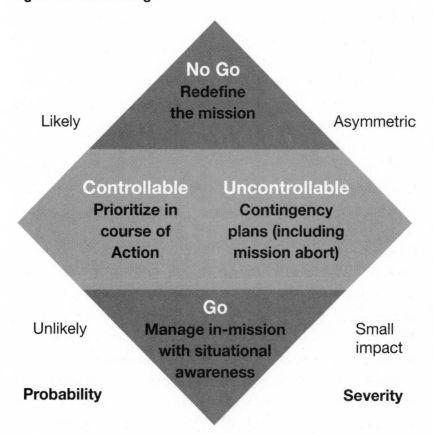

Source: Afterburner Inc.

STEP 3: IDENTIFY RESOURCES TO DRAW ON

Now you'll know your mission's objective, and the threats it faces. It's time to start marshalling your resources and plans to achieve that objective. Time to exercise those brains, bounce ideas off each other, go crazy with the sticky notes and the whiteboards. Again, a little bit of curiosity and imagination, and you may find you've got more to draw on than you think.

This stage is a quick pass on resources. Keep focus on the specific mission and its specific priority threats. You're about to develop a course of action, and each of its steps will prompt a need for resources and people, things tangible and intangible. What you miss now you'll pick up then. Get into the habit of thinking quickly yet expansively.

Push for ideas in two areas. First, *who* have you got to draw on—in your team, in your leadership and the support they can offer, in your organization, among your clients and relationships. What skills and expertize do you have there, and how do you access it? Second, *what* can you bring to the mission? What funding, spaces and places, plant and equipment, systems and technology, supplies and material?

Your organization will offer you more resources than you think. How do you know what's on offer? Know your business; know your organization. Walk around and see what's there. Volunteer for cross-business teams. Talk to people, listen to what they say. Understand what they do. Ask how *you* might be able to help *them* do their job more easily. That will help you understand what they do now, and what they can do in the future. You never know if that's a resource you may be able to draw on.

A situational awareness of your own organization will offer up more resources than you imagined you had. Those resources can be multiplied by considering people outside your own organization:

your clients, relationships, alliances, and communities. Your channel partners, as well as the specialist marketers within your organization. Any relationship you have is a potential resource. Everyone likes to be asked to do something, within reason. People like being in relationships where they can help each other in meaningful ways, not just talk about the weather. Be willing to help people, and they will be willing to help you.

With people come valuable resources, tangible and intangible. But you might want to run down the following checklist of tangible resources to see what you really have to hand. At this stage, you've considered your objective and threats, so it's best to have these squarely in mind when considering resources. Otherwise, you're free-forming a wishlist of things you may never need.

Your tangible resources will come from these categories: finance (money or exchange), technology, human capital, mechanical and business systems, equipment and tools, supplies and materials, land and facilities. Run through that list and consider whether anything you have access to will help you either meet your objective or beat your threats. Again, don't overthink it, as you'll have the chance to rethink resources when working through your course of action in Step 5.

STEP 4: EVALUATE LESSONS LEARNED

You'll know as well as we do that there's a big difference between data and knowledge, and between knowledge and wisdom. I may know some facts, and I may know how to do things that involve those facts. But am I wise enough to make the right decisions with that knowledge?

A fast-moving consumer goods company (FMCG) may have launched a thousand products over the years. Those launches may have involved a thousand people. That collective experience should hold all the data, knowledge, and wisdom the company would ever need—to add to their current market insights. But can they access that wisdom?

That's a nirvana that seems to have been beyond all but a few organizations—a knowledge system deep enough to hold what's needed, and simple enough to access it. Given the power of today's everyday database, computing and search engines, companies should be able to store knowledge in great quantities, and retrieve it easily. But they don't. As we'll see in Chapter 14, 'The Flex wings', the main reason is not that they can't build that store, but that their people don't demand it or look in it. People tend to work things out for themselves and reinvent the wheel. That's natural, and such curiosity and independence are welcome wherever time and money aren't so important.

With Flex, most of the lessons learned have come from the immediate past. Don't forget, each mission is debriefed and generates lessons learned for the very next mission, which become part of standard operating procedure then and there. But other lessons learned are for less common events and contingencies, and so need to be stored away in the standards to find later.

If time and resources are important to your organization, your team needs to dig out that deeper experience, and fast. Three questions will take you there:

1. What standards are *relevant*?
2. What *relevant* experience is there in the team?
3. What *relevant* experience can we tap into outside the team?

'Relevant' is the word here, especially for lessons from outside the team. As with resources, the lessons you're after are only those that will increase the chances of mission success or help you avoid a threat. You're tapping into a team that knows its business, and knows its history—it has situational awareness—so allow it to tap into its experience and memory.

One of the lessons that will almost always be relevant is to deal with the person, not only the facts. Serge learned that one early in his post-air force days. He was representing an electronics company in a sale to a government entity, and knew that their solution was far and away the best on offer. It was terrific engineering and software that was sure to do the job needed, at the right price. But Serge hadn't spent the time needed with the people making that decision. He hadn't spent time with them at all—which meant he'd not given himself the chance to empathize with them as people, to appreciate their motivations, to understand their concerns on the deal, and to explain how his client's electronics met those concerns. He just thought that being the standout best option was enough to win the day. Fortunately, that was early in Serge's post-military career, and he's a quick learner. It's a lesson that resonates through the planning of any deal he now does.

More well-known across the pharmaceutical and FMCG industries is the Tylenol lesson. In October 1982, seven people in Chicago died after taking Tylenol capsules, the then leading painkiller in the U.S. Someone had put cyanide in bottles on the supermarket shelves. Johnson & Johnson might have tried to deal with the emergency under cover. Instead, they removed and destroyed 31 million bottles nationwide, led the introduction of tamperproof packaging and caplets, and kept the public and authorities fully informed. In other words, they reinvested in their leadership of that particular market. It's a lesson of responsibility and success that still resonates. But keep your hunt for such lessons tight. You'll get another opportunity to think about them when you have your draft course of action laid out.

There is one lesson, though, we always keep at the top of the list—Hofstadter's Law:

'It always takes longer than you expect, even when you take into account Hofstadter's Law.'[3]

STEP 5: ASSIGN A COURSE OF ACTION

Here's where all the thinking from Steps 1 to 4 comes together in the actual plan or course of action. Getting to this plan reflects what Flex planning is all about: fast, yet considered; diversity in thought, yet a team. Similarly, the course of action reflects what Flex plans are all about: simple yet dynamic; direct yet empowering.

Is this process about nailing a plan in one hit? No. Planning is iterative. Each step suggests a threat, which requires an assessment, which demands a response. As each step is identified, you'll think of the resources and lessons to make that step a certainty rather than a hope. We'll get to contingency planning and Red Team reviews. It's all about testing and re-testing, to iterate and improve the plan, quickly and efficiently in the available time.

What is a course of action?

The course of action is essentially a simple three-column list that sets out a series of tasks, each assigned to an individual, to be done by a certain time: *who* does *what* by *when* (see Table 4). It includes decision points that may trigger different tasks or options, or allow tasks to be skipped. But it does not include *how* these tasks are to be done, nor state the obvious, nor restate standards.

A list of tasks

The team will need some form of logic to help identify tasks that, done together, will reach the mission objective. The military would think of the lines of operation that are needed. For example, if the day's mission was to take and hold an area of contested land, there would be tasks assigned to various combat, logistics, and communication units. But if the mission was to hold a large area of contested land with a big civilian population, the lines of operation might include counter-insurgency action, humanitarian

**Table 4: Clear course of action
(Create a data capture strategy)**

Who	What	By when
Paavan	Identify all relevant contacts and resources—R&D, legal, marketing, other	4 April
Marianne	Identify existing data strategy and roadmaps (e.g. from business unit, innovation team, marketing, consulting)	14 April
Ian	Complete document template and strategy (what customer data needed, and how it will be used)	25 April
Gabriela	Create draft materials (samples and business case) to share with units who will have to capture data (customer, sales, marketing, renewals)	5 May
Gabriela	Finalise roadmap to share materials with those units	5 May
Ian	Complete sharing of draft materials	15 May
Ian	Release final data capture systems for use	30 May

action, governance capacity, water infrastructure, telecommunications, shipping lanes—a whole host of responsibilities that need to be independently managed, yet have a common purpose. (You might imagine that each of these lines of operation looks like strategies directed towards a HD Destination, and you'd be right. The Flex approach is common no matter the team's level of effort.

Each of these lines of action might have its own course of action. But each will come down to a very limited number of tasks: up to a dozen tasks in that single list. A project manager might break down all of these tasks into component actions, and mark them out in a Gantt chart using specialized software, but that's the job for a project manager. This is a team course of action, and a single list will do. Simple.

Decision points on the timeline

A Flex plan is dynamic, which it won't be if it demands certain actions at certain times. There needs to be flexibility. We don't know everything at the planning stage: we don't know the effects of our actions, and don't know our competitor's every move. So we need decision points along the way, forks in the road that make us pause and consider.

There are three types of these decision points, each very different in nature but critical to the mission, that are part of the course of action: expected events, controllable threats that are realized, and regular team check-ins. Uncontrollable threats of course demand a contingency plan (Step 6):

1. **Expected events.** The first on the list are decisions to be made when we get to an expected point. A takeover target or raw material may have reached a trigger price point. The team is expecting to make that decision, and either has the information it needs to make it, or knows where to get it.

2. **Controllable threats.** The second set of decisions are triggered by threats that your plan hasn't yet controlled. You'll never really know the timing of these triggers, though you'll have an idea. Ideally, you'll have a lead indicator: something that says the threat is about to be realized. The share registry of your takeover target might show a surge in a competitor's holding: time to respond. If it's a threat you can control, you're still on your course of action.

3. **Regular team check-ins.** The third set of decision points aren't on the course of action, but are part of your plan. These are the team's check-in points, and their intervals make up the mission's execution rhythm. If your mission is staged to take

two months, you might be checking in weekly. If your mission is over in a day, you might check in every hour or so. The check-in might be a formal meeting—the X-Gap meeting we cover in Chapter 10, 'X-Gaps and execution rhythm (Keeping the plan to reality)'.

Let's say our four F-15s or F/A-18s are flying a mission in a combat zone. We expect to engage enemy bandits, and so need decision points leading up to the 'merge', the moment at which we would intercept the bandits on our current flight paths. The first decision point is an expected event that comes at 60 nautical miles (111 kilometers) out from the merger: we will declare the threat hostile and commit our force to the engagement. If four bandits are flying together, we will do the same and fly four abreast; if they split into two groups, we will do the same. The second decision point occurs at 40-miles (74 kilometers)-to-merge: we fly to higher altitude to maximize our missile capabilities. About 40 seconds later, at 20 miles (37 kilometers) out, we lock our missiles onto different targets, and launch them. Inside 20 miles, things get a little hectic, decision-making is compressed to seconds. My controller is telling me about other bandits I am yet to target, trying to sneak in while I'm committed to the first group. What range do they get to before I have to deal with them or 'pump out', turn away from this fight, buy some time, build in some distance between me and these two groups before 're-attacking'? We are constantly assessing: range, angles, my altitude, the bandits altitude, whether the radar is working properly. Am I targeted? Is that 'spike' (the indication of another jet's radar in the cockpit) from these bandits? Why is it coming from over there?

These decision points might occur twenty to 30 times in a half-hour mission. At each of these points, we need to know what the options are, who will make the decision, what information they need to do so, and who is providing that information. That decision point is an item on the course of action. The team has to be prepared for them, and the plan ensures they will be.

Process for creating the course of action

What you're aiming for is a course of action that is as clear as possible, for which each step is as simple as possible, and each step is assigned as an individual task. *Who* does *what* by *when*. To get there, one Flex approach when the planning group is large enough—say 9 or more people—is to split it into three groups working independently, then bring their thinking together.

Using three groups rather than planning the mission with the whole team together has a number of advantages. Everyone gets involved and contributes—you don't have the Type As hogging the air time, without perhaps more thoughtful team members having a say. You also have a greater chance of avoiding two common group errors. 'Groupthink' is the more familiar one: where everyone gets behind a poor plan because that's where the energy is, and nobody wants to stand in front of a rolling train with an alternative view.

Another example of groupthink is the Abilene Paradox, where somehow an entire group agrees on a plan that no individual actually wants. How would that ever happen?

Say you're all having a long lunch, it's the holiday season, the conversation is flowing, everyone is relaxed and could happily sit there all day. But somehow sitting in the one place all day doesn't seem the right thing to do, so someone asks whether they should get up and walk the mile down to the river to resettle at another favourite venue. It's a fair suggestion, but intended more as a half-hearted ponder than an actual vote. But everyone's in a good mood, so decide to go along with the new plan, even though they're *really* happy where they are. And so the party breaks up, people walk in pairs, the rowdy sharing of stories stops, prospective couples angle towards each other, and by the time you arrive at the afterparty you're only half the number you thought you were. You've moved from everyone being 100 percent happy to half the party being 50 percent happy and the other half being somewhere else. And all without realizing it. Yup, the Abilene Paradox strikes again.

So brief the whole team to prepare a course of action, before splitting them into three groups. Brief them by reviewing the first four steps: the mission objective, and its relevant threats, resources, and lessons. We want the three plans to be different. We are looking for creative ideas, options to overcome the same hurdle, different routes to the same endpoint.

Two of the groups take all of that briefing seriously: they must come up with a plan that addresses the identified threats, using the identified resources. The other is the 'blue sky' group, unconstrained by threats or resources or traditions or protocols, limited only by their imagination. Anything goes. A new light bulb will go on in this group almost every time. Recently, 'Sable' was working with a team from a New York-based flavors and fragrance company looking to get a new detergent accepted into African markets. The two serious groups thought through the standard path of distributors, agents, and logistics, as though the continent were somewhere in the Americas. The blue sky group remembered some cautious tales from previous attempts by Western companies to introduce household products to Africa. So they suggested sending a 'deep dive' team in to live with an African family and find out how families might actually use detergent of any type, and their own detergent in particular. It sounds simple, but being launched into blue sky also helps free a team up from their standard methods and assumptions.

The final step is to resolve the three plans into one plan that the team will support. The mindset here is not to select the best plan, but to create a single plan from the best ideas of the three. Each team presents their plan to the other groups, so that the nature and purpose of each step is clear. To start, choose the easiest to read, cleanest, most comprehensive plan—usually one of the 'constrained' plans. Mark its tasks as an action (A), a contingency (C) or delete (X). Switch to the next plan, and work through its steps to see if anything can be added to the first (A or C), or if any of the existing steps could be altered, or their order changed. Then the same for the third plan. Finally, have a look at the resulting final plan, to consolidate and clean up the steps, and see what gaps or threats remain.

Red Team review

It would be a remarkable achievement for your team to come up with the perfect plan for a complex mission in a single planning session. It's a difficult task, made more difficult by the inherent tendency for teams to rely too much on their own knowledge, and be a little too optimistic on the outcomes. That's particularly the case when a team really likes a plan, can imagine it happening, and almost taste its success. They've bought into it, have sunk their emotional capital into it—and will be blind to its threats. That's a part of what Daniel Kahneman calls the 'inside view' in his ground-breaking book *Thinking, Fast and Slow*.[4]

You guessed it. What you need is an outside view. Instead of launching the plan and later having a post-mortem on its marginal success, have a fresh set of external eyes test it out thoroughly before you start. They'll think of threats you won't think of, and test that the whole plan rests on a baseline of realistic data and assumptions. Remove the planning fallacy of optimism. Bring in the Red Team.

The Red Team has had a long history in the U.S. military. Most recently and famously, it was used in planning the successful Navy SEAL raid on Osama Bin Laden's hideout at Abbotabad—Operation Neptune Spear. An entirely independent, outsider's view of a strong yet risky plan made it that little bit stronger and less risky. Blue versus Red has been combat language ever since the U.S. War of Independence and, up until World War I, War Plan Red was the U.S. strategy for any potential war against Great Britain, the most likely enemy throughout the nineteenth century. Happily, the UK Ministry of Defence now also employs Red Teams, without calling them blue.

Now, it's no trivial task to bring in a Red Team to critique a team plan, without offending the team or raising hackles that may take a while to ease down. It's a potentially confronting stage of planning, sometimes held under time pressure for the mission to get under way. So there are tested rules to amp up the value of the Red Team while minimizing background noise. They apply to Red Team identity and process.

The Red Team should consist of two to five people who are external to the planning team. They cannot be present in the game, but they need to be helpful, to want the mission to succeed. They need to know the context and implications of the mission, with experience in similar operations or markets—ideally with the differing perspectives of customer, competitor, vendor, regulator, etc. In our language, they should have situational awareness for the mission, and be able to suggest additional threats, resources, and lessons learned.

It's essential that the Red Team session is held in person or over a live video link. (Every time we've weakened that rule, or asked people just to 'look over a plan', it hasn't worked. If it's done remotely, there are just too many distractions, and the lack of focus makes the effort near pointless.) Hold the Red Team session in a room with minimal distraction, so that the focus is on the plan and the plan only. Have two of the planning team ready as scribes. Brief the Red Team on what's needed from them: alternative perspectives on the assumptions, actions, threats to and effects of the mission. The planning team leader presents the plan visually—in charts and writing—the team leader guiding the Red Team through it, but not talking over their reading and thinking. Then wait.

The Red Team should ask the clarifying questions they need, then offer comments in rotation, one after the other, until they have no further comments to offer. The two scribes work in rotation also, so as not to miss anything when the comments flow quickly. Each comment is offered with the phrase 'Have you considered . . . ?' That is the question. This session is not a debate over whether or not the plan is a good one. There is no place to either attack or defend the plan. It is only to consider additional thoughts on the mission's assumptions, actions, threats, and effects. There is only one comment in response: 'Thanks.'

After the Red Team is thanked and dismissed, the mission team addresses each comment in turn and adjusts the course of action if needed. That's all it is. The term 'Red Team' has taken on a lot of specialist meanings for organizations and individuals who 'specialize' in red teaming. But in Flex, its role and commitment is very simple. We are just looking for an unbiased, experienced, valued opinion. There is no preparation or specialist expertize needed. Just be at the planning room for the Red Team session.

STEP 6: CONFIRM CONTINGENCY PLANS

By now, the only thing you haven't planned for is the threats that you cannot control. Now it's their turn. Your team needs to be able to answer every *what-if* it can think of, and be ready to respond to it. Respond is the word, not react. Having thought of responses, you are already ahead of changing conditions. If you have to react to unknowns in real time, you are already behind.

As pilots, we work the what-ifs hard, to be one step ahead in an action. What if the weather changes over the target area after we're airborne? What if the air refuelling tanker doesn't show up? What if a ground force needs our assistance more urgently than we need to take out our target? We like to say that flexibility is the key to air power, and preparation is the key to flexibility. In fact, because we know our standard procedures so well, and we know the likely plan for most missions, about 50 percent of our planning time is spent on these contingencies.

Your contingencies will be just as challenging. What if one of your team hasn't turned up? What if your morning flight is fog-delayed? What if one of your audience takes offense, or is just grumpy, and really starts to interfere with your meeting? It's much easier to brainstorm these possibilities beforehand than it is walking up to the client site in a heatwave with an armful of materials, or facing a boardroom of hostile investors, or a conference hall of alarmed employees. Much better then to know exactly what to do, and do it as coolly and calmly as possible. That's impressive stuff. Every client and employee loves someone who has thought ahead to cover things beyond their control.

Practice contingency plans carefully

You'll know that these are not fanciful possibilities. Stuff happens. A product launch and the star celebrity doesn't turn up. Who or what's going to take their place? Is it a fill-in celebrity, a cross-over to a live feed, or a product launch that doesn't depend on a celebrity? Keep peeling back what could go wrong, until there's nowhere else to go.

Importantly, be ready for your contingency responses even more automatically than your expected course of action. Learn them, practice them, remember them. Why? Because a contingency that hits is almost by definition a potential disaster, and that disaster will be playing on your mind. You've done all this hard work and planning, and now it's on the line. Your team's on the edge of panic, and only its contingency planning will hold them steady.

In 1991, Murph was in mock-dogfight in the 128th Fighter Squadron, when the two jets attacking him rammed into each other, in mid-air. There it was, an ordinary day's training, and two jets had hit each other. A one-in-a-million emergency, with dire consequences for two guys Murph knew well. But all pilots are briefed on that emergency from the day they start flying fighters. Do not fly under the last known altitude of the collision. Do not under-fly a parachute. Mark the position of the mid-air and the winds aloft for the rescue team, and keep clear.

So what happened on that morning of 15 January? Murph shut out what the mid-air could mean and put his body and mind into autopilot. He executed a scripted contingency plan that he never expected to need. He went through the procedures step-by-step, and helped save the life of a great fighter pilot. It was automatic, and critical.

Contingency–trigger–action

To be ready for a what-if, Step 6 asks you to clearly define three things:

1. the contingency, or uncontrolled threat
2. its trigger—when you know that the threat has become real, and
3. your action—what your team will do in response.

Most threats will have two triggers: a lead indicator that warns you the threat is likely, and a lag indicator to announce it's arrived. You *must* have a response to a lag indicator, and a response to a lead indicator is 'most advisable'. Again the weather provides a simple example. Rain is a potential threat for a sales event. Your lead indicator is a 24-hour forecast that it will bucket down. Start putting your alternative plans on stand-by. Your lag indicator is the rain itself. Too late to think of what to do then. Lucky you already have.

Contingency planning is nothing new for operations that deal with physical goods. A freight company knows that a substantial rise in fuel prices can wipe out an entire profit margin, and will have contingency plans in place. A lead indicator might be the news that national or regional crude inventories are falling, so the company acts by increasing its tier pricing by 0.1 percent weekly, explaining the move to its customers. The sudden outage of a critical refinery may mean that there is no such lead indicator, that the price of diesel fuel instantly rises by 25 percent. It's too late and too slow to ratchet up prices with that kind of lag indicator, so you have to take instant action: for example, a freight surcharge for non-metropolitan deliveries to help recover costs.

8

BRIEF (PUTTING YOUR PLAN INTO ACTION)

For a team to fly well, its leader must brief the team and each individual on it. Each individual must know without a shadow of a doubt what to do at each decision point, and what to do if something goes wrong. They must be able to visualize their part in the plan, before they go out to deliver it. That's why pilots say 'brief the plan, and fly the brief'.

Does that happen in business? Rarely. When a plan is formed or delivered from on high, people are expected to just work out their individual roles. With Flex, the team leader delivers the brief with the same care and preparation as the mission itself—because it is the mission! A room is set up for the purpose—a microclimate for success—with the mission's possibilities laid out. The team leader confirms the mission's objectives and why it matters, reviews the situation, confirms the standards that apply, and lays out simply and clearly who does what and when, why and what-if. Everything is scripted. Nothing is left to chance. And, most importantly, the team leader checks that each individual knows and understands their brief.

This is not to say that everything will go as planned and briefed. That glorious day is yet to arrive. But whatever happens, each team member will be prepared for it.

THE LAST ROUNDS OF PLANNING

We don't need to tell you that the real world is not as neat as the steps laid out in this book. People don't leave the planning room and walk back in to be briefed. Nor do they stride out to execute their mission. There is a time gap between the formal planning process and the brief, and the team spends that gap updating and nailing the plan. New data, new possibilities, and new situations will each prompt you to reconsider some element of the plan. In fact, the plan is only finalized in the acts of writing it up and delivering it as the brief. That is when all the possibilities being considered by the team leader have to be crystallized into a single, clear, coherent course of action. It has to be laid down, and it has to be convincing.

Tom and Boo kept honing their plans for CTG Global for eighteen months before finally launching into Afghanistan. Were they poor planners and procrastinators, unwilling to take the plunge? No. They just knew that working in a country that at best could be described as 'in reconstruction' and at worst as the contested territory of rival warlords was not something you took on lightly. And they were working on those plans in the evenings after their day jobs. When they were finally ready to bring their strategy to life, they switched to CTG full-time, finalized and planned, briefed themselves on their first daily mission, and continued their daily cycle of plan–brief–execute–debrief for the next four years.

THE BRIEF IS THE MISSION

Ask a business person how their mission went, they'll answer 'Fantastic, so good. It was amazing how . . .'—whatever the result. When a sportsperson comes off the field and gets trapped by the roaming mike, they mumble something through exhaustion about a tough game, played hard, did well. Ask a fighter pilot how their mission went, and they'll want to reply, 'We executed the brief.' That's it. In their minds, the mission is so tightly tied to the brief, that executing the brief is their finest achievement. In their world, in the Flex world, *they brief the plan and fly the brief.* They would no more fly a mission without a brief, than go to work naked.

We're not kidding that the mission is the brief. Sure, one is a mental picture in advance, the other is the actual doing. But they have to merge in the mind. That brief is your transition between planning and doing. Before the brief, there is a lot of possibility and nervousness. After it, everyone knows exactly what to do and how they will do it as a team. That's a real psychological bridge that must be crossed. Not everyone makes it. In his poem, 'The Hollow Men', T.S. Eliot talks of the shadow that falls between conception and creation. You do not want to stay in that shadow.

In our work with clients, people will attend a brief and still be questioning whether the plan will work. It's really too late for that questioning now. If there are doubts occupying precious space in the mind, it will lead to task saturation during the mission. You've stayed in Eliot's shadow for way too long. The brief is the cut-off: time to stop doubt, stop uncertainty, stop planning, and start executing. Alignment and accountability gets drilled in right here.

People who question a brief may be forgetting that a team's work is a *social* rather than a personal activity. States of mind and relationships between people *matter*. Donald Sull from MIT talks about the social dynamics as a team moves towards executing a mission.[1] People are doing things because others are doing them: just like we will jump into a river when our team does, but would not on our own. People are making commitments to each other that are personal and binding. They need to be making the same set of commitments if the mission is to start on the right note.

THE LEADER'S BRIEF

So the brief is not just a ceremony and certainly not just another meeting. It has to be done well for the mission to be done well. It is unique in many ways. Notably, it is the *only* one-way communication that takes place in all of Flex. The team leader is no longer facilitating, they are delivering. The leader has control. It is the leader's time to set his or her style, and to reinforce the expected team culture and standards.

It is true that not many team leaders want to take advantage of this moment. They may not want to appear to micromanage, they may not have the confidence, they may not *appear* to have the ability. If that is you, remember why Flex briefing is different. It comes after Flex planning, which the whole team has taken part in. The mission plan that's being briefed is the team's plan and the team's mission. You know it's not micromanaging, because you're reminding the team of the roles they've accepted, not telling them what to do. You know that the team believes it's a good plan, because it has been theirs in the making. This isn't about you, it's about the mission. You're just the means to the team's end.

And yet, you are now assuming accountability for the mission, which you'll keep if it is a failure, and share if it is a success. The team members will respect that responsibility, as divided authority at this point will destroy not only the mission, but the team. The brief marks that point and that respect for that authority. The leader is accountable for the role of leading their mission, and the team is accountable for their roles in it. Good followership is as critical as good leadership.

At the end of George Clooney's briefing of the heist in *Ocean's Eleven*, a team member asks the obvious question: if we get past security, through the locks, into the cage, down the elevator, past the armed guards, into the vault, invisible to the cameras and get the cash . . . we just walk out untouched? A pause from Clooney as Ocean, then 'Yeah.' 'Oh . . . [nod] . . . OK.' Respect for Ocean's authority has been expressed.

We'd be surprised if you've seen a brief that effective, and if you have it's unlikely to have been in your boardroom or office. Typically, the more dangerous the mission, the more precise the brief. In hospitals, surgeons and head nurses are becoming more and more meticulous in their pre-operation team briefings. Outside the military or surgeries, most of us don't see that. We're left to see movie scenes, or coaches' pre-game briefings, or the wishful thinking of middle managers cast as motivational excess, or the desperate hopes of families planning a road trip. So what we want to get across to you is the need for clean, clear, precise communication—as a Flex brief. You won't find it on YouTube.

THE RIGHT BRIEFING MICROCLIMATE

The precision and authority you need from your brief is not going to happen by accident. The tone of your mission will be set by its brief: both by its setting and its conduct. A sloppy brief will lead to a sloppy mission, nothing surer. It is the time and place to show that, as leader, you are well-prepared, the plan is well-designed, and you are confident of its success. If you're serious about the mission, be just as serious about the brief. Prepare yourself. You're now in execution mode.

That starts with where the brief takes place. It has to be absolutely free of distraction. The military have rooms that are used only for briefs and debriefs, which may not always be possible in the workplace. If you're using a project 'war room', clean it up. If you're in a nice modern meeting room with glass windows or walls, draw the curtains. The only thing anyone wants to see is the team, the printed plans, any visual charts and models, and you. Keep it clear and simple, with presentation slides at an absolute minimum.

Be early. Be meticulous. Check that the whiteboard pens are working. Print out what you need for each person, and place it together on each place setting. Tell your team when they enter the room not to touch anything until you tell them: you don't want them distracted and reading ahead and missing something important. Get everyone to turn their phones off. Be bold, if a member of the team refuses, tell them you aren't prepared for them to be part of your mission.

Don't listen to those who question the need for this, yourself included. The rest of the team must be there five minutes early. If they're not five minutes early, they're late. This is not something to be squeezed in between phone calls. It is the point of the day; time to switch on.

Your tone will be confident and positive. You know your stuff, so you can keep steady eye contact with the whole team—not flitting about, not staring at one person. Work through the whole brief, holding questions to the very end. Vary your speed and tone to keep your delivery interesting. But it's not a long speech, it is a concise, systematic brief. Your team can handle it.

The most important microclimate for your brief is the one that settles between your ears. You have to be ready to brief, and to brief well. What you brief will be your team's plan, and it has to work. Fighter pilots do something to make sure they know their plan and that the plan works. Almost without exception, we sit down and *visualize* the mission, action by action. Athletes do it too, visualizing their moves and those of their competitors. You can call it 'visualization', as the athletes do. We call it chair-flying. (Yes, we know.)

Just as we chair-fly the mission, we chair-fly the brief. The value of doing that beforehand cannot be overemphasized. Answer your own questions before both the mission and the brief are set in stone. Get to the briefing room early, and chair-fly the brief you're about to give. Try it out. Before you make your next important call, chair-fly it. What questions will they ask? What are your answers? Chair-fly your next conference call or presentation, visualizing what each person is going to say, and how they'll say it. Chair-fly *everything*. Enjoy.

B-R-I-E-F THE PLAN

It won't surprise you that the content of your brief is almost exactly the same as your planning session. The results of your mission planning are translated into the parts of the brief. However, the intent and time spent on the brief is very different. Where in mission planning you're exploring the steps, in briefing you're declaring them. Alone or with your team, you have now reconciled any disagreements or uncertainties in the planning process. This is now the plan!

As clearly as possible, work through your BRIEF: **B**ig picture; **R**estate (mission objective); **I**dentify (threats and resources); **E**xecute (your course of action); and **F**lexibility (the contingencies).

If you think that sounds like the steps in your mission planning, you'd be right. One way Flex keeps things simple is by repeating the same pattern of thoughts in the plan, the brief, the execution, and the debrief. Run through the mission planning steps if it's easier to remember, but we like to B-R-I-E-F the plan.

Big picture

Here is the time to confirm why this mission even exists: your organization's High-definition (HD) Destination and the strategy, organizational culture, and identity to get there. The team has to have that situational awareness (which we'll explore in Chapter 12, 'Situational awareness'). It has to know what this mission, if successful, will support. That way, if any decisions are to be made on the fly, they can be done with the right effects in mind.

Having the big picture firmly in mind makes all the difference when the team has a discretion to exercise, which will be often. In May 2009, Lance Corporal Rolando Cabezas was on a regular field mission in Farah, Afghanistan. His unit came across a farmer digging an irrigation ditch beside the road. At the time, the U.S. Army and its Australian and European allies were losing soldiers to IEDs (Improvised Explosive Devices) buried under transit roads. Being found by a U.S. Army unit while digging under the road placed the farmer in great danger.

Yet Lance Corporal Cabezas didn't jump to conclusions, didn't shoot and ask questions later. He used the few Pashto phrases he knew, and confirmed that the farmer was just farming. And he knew the bigger picture. General Stanley McChrystal had seen that to beat the Taliban in Afghanistan, the Allied forces needed to win the trust of the Afghan people. That wasn't easy in a country that had seen foreign armies opposed to their own warlords continually since the Soviets invaded in late 1979. The U.S. soldiers needed to win the hearts and minds of the people they were there to protect.

So Lance Corporal Cabezas stationed a patrol to protect the farmer, took off his helmet and helped to dig the ditch. Word of the action spread far, through the Afghan district and beyond to *The Wall Street Journal* and to this book. That one deed did more to advance the peacekeeping mission in Afghanistan than any planned mission that day. It was so effective, the farmer invited the U.S. Marines into his village and declared them 'sons of the village' for their generosity.

Contrast how an ill-used discretion can undermine a desired brand, culture, and strategy. You will know as many stories as us. One of our favourites goes back almost a century. In the 1930s, the Maharaja of Alwar visited London, and happened on a Rolls Royce showroom while on a casual stroll. Having at one time 24 Rollers at home in Rajasthan, he went in to investigate the newest models. The salesman made the wrong assumption about a casually dressed sub-continental in his shop, and ushered him quickly out. The non-plussed Maharaja returned that afternoon in full dress and entourage, and ordered six cars, paying for their delivery to Alwar. The unwitting salesman was very pleased.

Back home, the Maharaja unpacked his six gleaming motors from their delivery crates . . . and sent them with a few of his old ones to be used as garbage trucks. Word spread. In Europe and America, the boast of a new Rolls Royce owner was met with friendly chiding: 'Oh, the garbage truck of India!' The damage to the carmaker's brand and sales was significant, threatening its recovery from the 1930s Depression. No social media in sight, no postings on the web, no viral flaming, just a hit to the company when it needed it least.

Every day, every mission, is a chance to go one step closer to (or drop two steps back from) your HD Destination.

Restate the mission objective

Restate the mission objective, checking for yourself and for others that it is clear, measurable, achievable, and aligned. Don't assume that people know it. It's worth restating it. Meet their gaze and check that they know it! It lets everyone know that nothing major has changed since finalizing the plan or, if it has, what has changed.

In doing this, restate how the mission objective aligns with the organizational objectives. In Chapter 13, 'Flex in organizations', we talk about the HD Destination we're all aiming for, and the long-term strategy that will take us there. Every mission and action in that strategy will have an effect on the team, on the organization and on its environment—all part of the one system. At one infrastructure client, we kept asking teams to restate how the effects of the immediate mission would take them closer to its long-term objectives. Team leaders would often resist, not wanting to spend even twenty seconds on that additional context. But that laid down the 'why' of the mission. The team had to know *why* this mission was important. And our consistent feedback from the teams themselves was that they weren't always clear how their mission fitted into their bigger picture.

Identify your threats and resources

This stage is really to touch on any *specific* intelligence that is likely to be highly relevant to your mission, whether or not it was covered in the planning stage. It includes the major threats you've identified and the resources you've prioritized in your planning. And it extends to the relevant organizational, market, economic, and physical environment in which you're operating.

Start by listing the top threats the team will have to keep an eye out for, and the major resources that will help it reach its objective. It's a recap not a discussion, just enough for the team to have enough situational awareness to make the right decisions.

Execution—who does what by when

This is where three-quarters of your briefing time is spent, the reason the team is in the room. What we have to do to get the mission done. This is your course of action—a clear, methodical listing of the actions that the team will take. Each action is owned by a single individual, who understands that it is his or her responsibility alone. Yet all the team knows what each other is doing. They all know how those actions will interact with their own, and therefore how they can support each other as wingmen.

The aim is to make it all simple. Remember, in a fighter squadron, flight leaders don't want their pilots to have to think very hard when they're engaged in combat. They want their minds as clear as possible for the actual engagement, to focus on the planes and missiles they're up against, and not on remembering their next step in the mission. Part of the course of action and the brief will be the timing for X-Gaps, the regular team check-in for any changes to the plan.

The best briefs take the form of a simple decision timeline. For example, say the jets are en route to the target. At five minutes out, they'll arm their weapons. At two minutes out, if all looks good, the flight leader will call them to commit and head in. But these are decision points, not yet actions. If the operating conditions are not right, then the flight leader will make the decision to adjust or abort the mission. All this is scripted before take-off, laid out on the decision timeline, and briefed point by point. *The pilots don't know what will happen, but they do know what they'll do when it does.*

There is no rocket science in this brief. But in business, if a team's day or week is briefed at all, it is rarely done with the deliberate care of the military. A direct result is that things are done with less confidence and consistency. Even if there is a plan, specifics will be overlooked, or held to when the operating conditions should dictate that they're dropped. The right actions aren't taken for the conditions, or in response to the day's events.

Flexibility—ready for contingencies

Finally, the Flex brief covers the uncontrollable threats to the desired course of action—what to do when things go wrong. Remember that the plan covers controllable threats in the course of action itself: minimizing the chances that something goes wrong. But how many plans call for a team member to do something, yet are silent on what happens if a third party doesn't deliver their piece, or the required data is unavailable? At the end of the brief, clearly restate what you determined in planning: the threat or contingency, the triggers that force a decision on that threat, and the actions that flow from those decisions.

Of these, the triggers are the most important to spell out for the team. They can check their plan to know what actions to take, but they have to recognize the trigger when it happens in real time! If the team is working on a property deal, there's always the threat that an unknown new party might enter the bidding. What event would signal that entry? How would the team recognize that trigger, and what should be your response?

A BRIEF'S LAST WORDS

The brief finishes with three things of equal importance: questions from the team, checking in that all is known and well, and a positive call to launch the mission. A brief that ends well is the right launchpad for your mission.

There are two simple rules for the questions: repeat the question before you answer so the whole team benefits, and never repeat something negative. If the question has a tinge of doubt to it, confirm it as a positive. Remember Clooney: are we just going to walk out with $150 million in cash. Yeah!

A brief delivered is one thing. A brief absorbed is another. How you check that your team knows exactly what it has to do is a question of personal style. Some will eyeball each person in search of any lack of conviction. Some will ask questions of the room and of the person. The RAAF technique is to *pose* a question, *pause* for a response, then *pounce* on one person for the answer. Lee Marvin in *The Dirty Dozen* pointed to the escape site's miniature model and had the team chant through each of the sixteen steps. Each to their own!

And a closing call to arms? Well, that's entirely a matter of personal choice. You know your team and what they need to hear better than we ever could. In Australia, little is said; in the U.S. a little more. As fighter pilots we put these words in the same category as leaving our homes on a tour: you never know if they may be the last ones between people you care about. You'll remember *Hill Street Blues*, and its daily call to 'Be careful out there.' We know of sporting coaches who have charged through doors (hinges unscrewed in advance, of course) to finish off a pre-game 'brief'. Go soft or go hard, but be positive.

9

EXECUTE (KEEPING PEOPLE TO THE PLAN)

One reason that few plans survive contact with reality is that people are human and don't always stick to the plan. (The other reason, that reality changes, we consider in the next chapter.) People lose focus, get overwhelmed, *think* that the situation has changed when it hasn't really or, for whatever reason, they just make mistakes. Most often, that's due to task saturation— too much going on, too much interference and interruption for one mortal to manage. Alternatively, accidents happen when there's not really much going on, not enough to keep the mind active and focussed. Either way, you need to protect against that loss of focus, and keep people to the plan. We've worked, for example, with a terrific sales team who supported each other to the hilt. Being millennials, they used live messaging for everything, sharing new leads and information, giving each other encouragement and congratulations—a stream of positive reinforcement and useful data. Yet when they sat back and looked at what was happening, they realized the cost of that interaction may have outweighed the positives. Yes, the new information was coming 'live', but was it distracting them from their immediate task? Yes, they were responding to each other and changing their course in real time, but was that thoughtful or reactive?

HOW PEOPLE LOSE FOCUS

We all know what it feels like to be overwhelmed, to lose focus on doing the important things, even to lose track of what the important things are. Our minds just can't take it all in. Surprisingly, though, it's more common for us to experience lack of focus when our minds are, quite literally, bored from inactivity. No matter how good a book or a film or a storyteller is, you might find your mind drifting off to other thoughts. That's because your mind can absorb information far more quickly than the speed of normal reading or speech. So the trick is to feed the mind just enough information for it to be fully engaged, yet not overwhelmed. That way, you can avoid both the sophomore and the saturation risks.

The sophomore risk

Sometimes, people who ought to know better just aren't paying enough attention to what's going on. Overconfidence leads to cut corners, false assumptions or just bad judgments. Research into air force accidents reveals a curious statistic. Errors are more likely to be made by pilots with four to seven years' experience—not the new or ageing pilots you might expect. Take a look at Figure 11. Pilots are building up their skills and experience all the time: the dotted line. Unfortunately though, their confidence and lack of focus rises even more steeply: the curved line. When they begin, they're fully engaged in the new experience, and can make quite good decisions while facing very new situations: what many call 'rookie smarts'. But from four years in, they're in a danger zone—until they come to their senses and again realize you have to pay attention if you're flying a 45,000-pound machine with

50,000 pounds of thrust at 1200 miles per hour. Maybe they've had a couple of close calls, maybe they learn from an error of a classmate—hopefully it wasn't fatal.

That's not so uncommon. We go through the same cycle at university. As a first year freshman, you're a little clueless and therefore cautious. Having survived that, you look down from the heights of second year at the new blood coming in. You're confident, cocky even. You're a sophomore—literally a 'wise fool' in ancient Greek. Same thing at work—come in and we're eyes wide open, looking for opportunities, for traps, and for assurance. As soon as we're comfortable, we start to take things a little too much for granted. We get called into line a couple of times, because for the first time our performance doesn't match our potential. But nothing's fatal, we can keep going. And if we do, the wisdom of experience kicks in and we can begin to lead.

Figure 11: Fighter pilot accidents most likely in years three to six

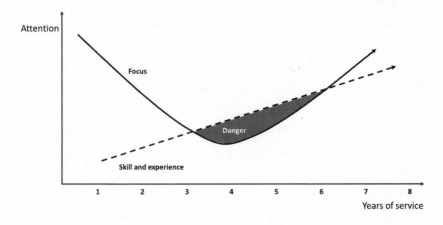

Source: Afterburner Inc.

The saturation risk

The standout, biggest risk to flawless execution—to any execution—is what pilots call the silent killer: *task saturation*. It is totally avoidable and insidious by nature. You have to watch out for it, to be able to recognize it, and to respond.

Task saturation is the *perception* that you have too much to do, in not enough time, with not enough tools or resources. Whether that feeling is real or imagined doesn't matter. Once it takes hold, you will not act the way you and your team need you to. You will let someone down, or worse.

In business, too many people wear overwhelming 'busyness' as a perverse badge of honour. The all-nighter before the killer presentation. Being three places at one time—two virtual, one physical—with those in the room with you getting the least attention. The cross-continent flights to chase one more meeting, to make up for the problem that was someone else's fault. That's one hell of an important person right there. It feels good to be so valuable. No matter that as task saturation increases, performance decreases; that errors track saturation like ants track honey. Task saturation in business is a sugar hit; it's nothing to be proud of.

Pilots learn that lesson the hardest way of all, seeing a comrade and mate lose their life for no good reason. Murph lost two close friends who flew perfectly good jets into the ground. Didn't see it coming. They were good pilots, and if you asked them how they were five seconds before impact, you'd have got a smiling thumbs up. But they died task saturated, and never knew it.

Spotting task saturation

Understandably given the stakes, the U.S. military has done a lot of work into recognizing when someone is getting task saturated. The work wasn't necessary—pilots are asked what they do when they feel stressed, and consistently say the same thing—but it did hammer home the anecdotal. What do people do when they *feel* they have too much to do with the time and resources they have? First up, the good endorphins in our body kick in, and we feel good, energized, ready to climb that mountain and skip down the other side. It's a great feeling, but it lasts as long as this sentence. Before long, our bodies' natural ways of dealing with stress get oversaturated. The nervous tension locks you up, and you'll do one of three things: you shut down, you flitter from task to task, or you fix on one thing and one thing only. Trouble is not far away.

The first and most harmless coping mechanism is to shut down. You look at your desk, your emails, your to-do list, and just go blank. Anything else becomes more important, no matter how trivial, as long as it's not part of that mess. Go for a walk, visit the gym, do your monthly receipts, play a game on the smartphone. That's fine every now and again, we all need a break. You might even be happy about it, and walk about the office looking for a pointless chat or an evening drinks buddy. But when the next day ticks over with no change, check in with yourself—is this OK, or have you shut down? Any luck, someone will have already noticed. The one good thing about shutting down is that it's easy to spot.

Flitterers, on the other hand, are bad news. They're risky because they *act* busy but do little, and kill you while they're doing it. Everything they do is part of their job, and they're not shutting down. They're not waving that flag that says 'It's all too much for me'. But they're not doing anything important, and not finishing anything at all. Compartmentalizers are specialist flitterers, flitterers with form. Have you ever wanted to get everything in order? Just put everything into nice, neat, calming piles and lines while just beyond your vision the world is burning? Rearrange the deck chairs on the *Titanic*?

Compartmentalizers will make lists, re-plan their project (again, by themselves), file papers, go from top to bottom, and become obsessively linear. Again, that's OK as a regular routine, keeping things in order so they never get out of control or need a year's cleanout. But if you're doing it when your team really needs you to be doing something else, then there is a problem. And the sign is that you're letting a team down in an uncharacteristic way: a missed deadline, a late arrival, or a communication that just doesn't make sense.

Finally, there are the channellers. As the name suggests, channellers have tunnel vision, focussed or fixated on one thing to the exclusion of all others. Most of us are potential channellers when things go wrong—80 percent of all people—and the examples are almost too many and too painful to recall. The cable company so determined to plant their new advertising campaign on the airwaves that they didn't think through whether their connection staff were able to meet the new demand. The day we just have to get something 'out the door', and close our ears and minds to any distraction, any phone call, any unplanned event that might interfere with getting the job done—and our sick child has been left at the training field for three hours, getting sicker by the minute. Too busy to make a phone call, you lose two days to care for him.

Flight 401

Nothing shows the destructive power of fixation more than the story of Flight 401. We have heard the black box audio a thousand times in our workshops, and still can't believe what we're hearing. On 29 December 1972, Eastern Airlines Flight 401 was approaching Miami International airport on a perfect, clear, windless night, with its full crew of three in the cockpit, and 176 people on board.

Ten miles (16 kilometers) out, the first officer says, 'Captain, let's put the landing gear down.' 'Roger.' The captain puts the landing gear handle into its down position, and looks to the three green lights that indicate that the right, left, and nose landing gear are down and locked, ready for landing. But only two indicators light up. They follow the emergency procedure checklist, and raise and lower the gear handle again. Again, just the two green lights.

The captain checks in with the Miami control tower, and puts the plane on a holding pattern at 2000 feet until they can sort out the landing gear indicator light. To better focus on fixing the light, they put the plane on autopilot. That's regular procedure and not a big deal—commercial airliners can land on autopilot if they have to.

The captain, co-pilot, and flight engineer then try to work out what's wrong with the indicator light, convinced that the landing gear is actually down, but just not showing on the instrument panel. They try everything—checking the hydraulic pressure, jiggling the light housing. For three minutes, the cockpit talk is all about the light. 'You got a handkerchief or something, so I can get a little better grip on this? Anything I can do it with? If I had a pair of pliers . . .' Finally, the captain directs the flight engineer to look down under the cabin for a visual. 'To hell with this. Go down and see if that red line is lined up down there. Don't screw around with that twenty-cent piece of light equipment.'

And still they keep fiddling with that twenty-cent light. But at some point, either pilot had leaned forward against the control yoke (steering wheel) with the five pounds (two kilograms) of pressure needed to disengage the autopilot. The plane had started a slow descent, not noticeable in the ink black night, over ink black water, when you're focussed on a single light on the instrument panel.

Miami control interrupts to check in: 'Eastern 401, how are things coming along out there?' As normal, the first officer checks the altitude and direction to respond. '1-8-0 . . . Hey, we lost some of the altitude here. We're still at 2000 right?'

Wrong. They were at 100 feet (30 meters). Still enough time for an alert pilot to react and pull the plane out. But for those last twelve seconds all three pilots were so task saturated that all their instincts were long gone. Captain: 'Hey, what's happening here?' And then the plane slams into the Everglades.

KEEPING PEOPLE TO THE PLAN

Whether it's task saturation or overconfidence, the result is the same: a lack of focus that can be fatal to missions, personal dreams, careers, and even lives. Pilots know that threat, and prepare for it as part of their plan. They use their checklists, focus on their central indicator, cross-check on the others, and use their wingmen. Wingmen check for blind spots and signs of task saturation, and pilots never go anywhere without a wingman. It's all part of their plan.

A dashboard, with primary (attitude) indicator and cross-checks

There are about 350 indicators in the cockpit of a fighter or a commercial jet. Nobody can keep track of 350 indicators. The answer is to be able to see four or five indicators clearly at all times, and if there's anything unexpected with them, start looking at the relevant others. Still, how would you or a business keep an eye on four, five, eight, or twelve indicators at a time? We would humbly suggest the dashboard layout of our cockpit (see Figure 12). It's been designed, tested, and improved over billions of flying hours by millions of pilots flying under direct combat, safety and commercial pressures. So it's worth a look.

The dashboard has all the indicators you need to see, in a hub-and-spoke layout. The center hub is the primary indicator. For pilots, that's the attitude indicator or 'artificial horizon'. If you can only do one thing, focus on this and adjust your wings to keep the plane level. (One look at the attitude indicator would have saved Flight 401.) The secondary indicators form the spokes. They're all important indicators of the plane's performance, so a

Figure 12: Classic aircraft cross-check dashboard

pilot will scan the dashboard constantly, and every scan passes over the center hub. It's the hub-and-spoke layout of the cockpit cross-check.

Many businesses use dashboards, but there are three standout features to the cockpit-style dashboard that aren't often seen. First, the primary indicator is the largest image and is at the center: you can't miss it. Second, all of the indicators are *visual*: You don't have to read anything when your eyes are rattling. You can quickly scan across the dashboard and see that the indicators are where they should be. Third and most importantly, if the indicators are not where you want them, you will know what you should *do* to adjust, correct, guide, and get the indicator back where it should be. For each dial, there is a corresponding action to take to move the needle.

At CTG Global, Boo and his partner Tom were creating a

new business from scratch. There is no off-the-shelf guide to managing people on humanitarian and infrastructure projects in war or war-recovery zones. In the earliest days, the only indicators that mattered were whether they were on plan, their cash in the bank, and the strength of their own relationship. Tracking the plan was the primary indicator, but their core assets were whether they were getting along well enough, with enough project cash, to see through to the next stage of the plan.

Once they secured their initial project—providing security for road building in Afghanistan—their reputation became a critical asset. But it was not something easily measured. Before long, they worked out one unexpected indicator of the health of their business that could reflect on almost all others: how well they looked after their staff, in particular how safe and well-fed they were. Keeping their staff safe and well-fed in such places meant that they got the best people by word-of-mouth, and that their people were loyal and worked hard. It meant that they were aligned with their clients: often humanitarian or aid agencies whose *own* stated objective was to keep people safe and well-fed. Keeping people safe and well-fed was the best single way to establish and protect CTG's reputation.

The Virginia Department of Transportation has a great public example of a dashboard, as one might expect with their responsibilities. Its ultimate test of success is what Virginians think about the job they're doing. That customer view is driven by their operational performance. So their Figure 13, Virginia DOT Dashboard, speaks for itself.

Your business will have its own key performance indicators, and these will make up the company's dashboard. Because it's the CEO's dashboard, it will show the CEO's priorities. Some dashboards will have the share price as the central attitude meter, others will have profit, or revenue, or margin, all depending on the company's current strategy and priorities. The main thing is

Figure 13: Virginia DOT Dashboard

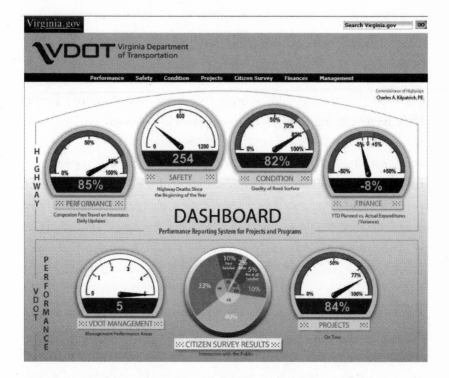

Source: See http://dashboardsbyexample.com/wp-content/
uploads/2012/03/vdot-transportation-dashboard.png.

that it is clear to the person using the dashboard what action to take to get the indicator level to where it should be.

Should everyone in the company be focussing on that dashboard? No. People at different layers and within different teams will have their own missions with their own objectives. The indicator that shows whether their own objective is being met should be that team's primary indicator. Other indicators should reveal factors that may contribute to that objective. The CEO's profit indicator, for example, may appear as a secondary indicator to be cross-checked, because that may reveal whether unbudgeted resources are available (or not) to help meet your objective.

Many companies want their employees to have one universal dashboard. But that implies everyone in the company should have the same priorities as the CEO. Would that distract them from their daily mission, the one they're assessed and paid on? You bet. Keep it on the side, but not center. It's not their priority.

Use your wingman!

Without a doubt, the most important way for you to keep focus on your plan is to have a wingman. Literally, two minds, two sets of eyes and ears, looking out for each other. Call it mutual support, call it a double act, call it whatever you want that doesn't imply a guy in a plane alongside you . . . just have one.

You will have seen the benefits of having two people at a meeting. You hear more things; when one person is listening hard, the other can be preparing; you have more energy in the room. When two people go to a meeting, they are far more likely to plan ahead for it, to consider the threats and contingencies; you can play roles, negotiate better, follow up with more enthusiasm.

Many executives have also experienced the benefits of a true working partnership, or at least a very clear and trusted second-in-command or 2IC to take over the reins whenever needed. The U.S. teamwork software company Atlassian is the latest to have benefited, with co-founders Scott Farquhar and Mike Cannon-Brookes sharing the CEO role from the firm's start up days to its 2016 listing on the New York Stock Exchange. They share the workload and the stress of building a business, take the breaks they need, and one of them is always there. Someone who can step in for you whenever needed is just as valuable, eventually, to lead in their own right.

Fighter pilots take that strength further. We don't go anywhere—anywhere—without a wingman. We don't fly a mission, we don't go out at night, and we don't take on important roles or personal missions without having someone by our side. In our mission teams, wingmen are easily identified. Beyond that, a wingman may be the life partner in our family or our formal business partner. It may equally mean someone who we share experiences with, or someone we work alongside in our work or personal communities. You know each other's roles and objectives, you know the threats to those objectives, and you know how you can support and rely on each other.

So this mutual support is less an action item and more a mindset that people in the team share. It starts with that old friend situational awareness, an idea that holds throughout Flex and that we explore fully in Chapter 12. Yes, there is that mission awareness, about the environment and potential external threats to the mission, but there's also an awareness about the person you're supporting: their fears and motivations, critical tasks, and what will make or break them. Without that awareness, you're an observer rather than a wingman: not a bad thing, but not what's needed.

Wingmen are not always someone physically close. So many people are out there on the road these days—pushing deals, sales, development, investments, research—and it's especially important for them to have wingmen. Truck drivers, couriers, and cabbies also typically work solo, on days that can be as frustrating or tiring as they are long. Groendyke Transport and Sears Home Services are two American organizations which found that the most natural wingmen for their drivers were their dispatch operators. These experts knew what the drivers were doing (or should have been doing) at all times, had the personal skills to check in every now and then with a banter or a more direct question, and the technology to hand to follow the drivers' progress. Their experience has been that a little investment in giving their dispatchers more time for each driver paid off in more reliable deliveries, happier drivers, and fewer accidents.

It's one thing to be aware of something, another again to say something. The U.S. Coast Guard has studied the causes of 389 marine casualties in 1998–99. In 68 percent of cases, it wasn't that the critical information wasn't available or known. It was that either the people who had the information didn't recognize its importance, and so the need to share it with others, or assumed that the others already had the information.[1] Some call this the 'common knowledge effect', so common everyone assumes everyone else knows it, but most are wrong. Overcoming this issue is part of the Flex mindset: don't be shy in speaking up if you see something that may be a problem.

You might have noticed by now that 'defensiveness' has no place in a Flex mindset. If you think speaking up in a team room or partnership is hard, try it in surgery. That's where the line holds firmest: 'Make sure you all let me know if you see me do anything dumb, different, or dangerous.' 'See something—say something,' you might say.

Clear, concise and certain communication

There are times for chewing the fat, and teams love them. But not when everyone's under pressure to perform. When there's a lot going on, a lot of it uncertain, you can't afford long rambles and you can't afford short statements that are unclear. Clear, concise statements also help you and those around you to keep focus. Ramble on, and people switch off. No matter how important your message, it won't be heard. And you may be taking up the time or phone line for more critical stuff.

Everything has to be clear, concise and certain. That's especially the case when people are tired or under stress. The Cold War movie *The Bedford Incident* is the classic warning example. Captain Finlander had taken the USS *Bedford* on a long, exhaustive hunt for a Soviet submarine, and at the critical point insists that 'if he fires one, I'll fire one'. Those last two words were heard by a tired crewman as an order to 'fire one', the anti-submarine rocket. Off it goes, to be answered by four nuclear-armed torpedoes and the end of the *Bedford*.

The other challenge is that as much as 80 percent of human communication is nonverbal: the tone, gestures, body position, and facial expressions. That's the value of a face-to-face meeting, or being in each other's line of sight when you're on an operation. So if you don't have those visual clues, you really need to get the tone and words right, over the phone or on the page.

There are some clear rules that can help keep your communication and minds on mission as follows:

1. **Work with hard data, not assumptions.** When task saturation is hitting you, it's amazing how an opinion or assumption can morph into a 'fact' on which other people's decisions are based. 'How long have we got?' can have only two answers: a number, or, 'I will find out.' If someone then wants your opinion, they'll ask.

2. **Your own jargon is OK.** What is convenient shorthand within the team may well be jargon outside it, but the team should still use it. Pilots use terms like 'inbound' to mean 'I'm on my way, on time, with no issues', or 'tumbleweed' to mean 'I have absolutely no situational awareness, and something bad could happen any time soon', or 'ballistic' to mean 'I am out of control and something bad *will* happen any time soon—stay away!' That assumes, of course, that everyone knows what it means: it is part of the team's language, part of its standards. Technical terms weren't made up to be vague or confuse people. They are created to describe a specific thing in context, more efficiently than before. In the military, those terms are chosen so that when used in the same situation they don't *sound* the same. We reduce the chance of mishearing someone, of making mistakes because of an

accent or a crackling line. So, 'commit/abort', or 'affirmative/ negative' rather than 'yes/no', which are so short they might be lost in a crackling line.

3. **Cut the chatter.** Fighter pilots support each other by saying only what they have to say, no more, and then get off the radio. That keeps ideas clear and lines free. In business and at home, in most situations, that may come across as abrupt. But remember we're talking about communication within a team that is focussing on a mission. If you're on a family road trip and it's time to turn off the highway, just make the call!

4. **Decide on simple patterns for both one-way and two-way communication.** For example, in two-way communication, agree on how to check you've made contact, that the other person is listening, and that they have heard you. Pilots aren't shy in asking for a 'repeat back' to make sure the word has got through: not the whole sentence, but a core word, phrase, or paraphrase. Similarly, agree on a simple structure for one-way communication like emails, if they're more than one line. Put the point of the email and the desired action at the top, and structure everything else below. If it's information about an event or process, use your friends 'who, what, and when'. Set your own rules, whatever they are, and stick to them.

Shed extra tasks

It has always taken self-discipline to stay focussed through our daily cacophony of personal and work plans, meetings, calls, and emails. That's even harder now that we have a glued-to-hand smartphone with its world of alerts, distraction, and temptation. So it's become ever more critical to be able to cut through that task list, and shed whatever you don't really have to do, now.

Most time-management approaches follow similar themes, and Flex is no exception. We set that out below, but if you prefer your own, go with that. The real difference is with Flex you have wingmen, there to help keep you focussed, shed tasks, and do the tasks you can't. If you need to, work with your wingman to problem solve how to shed tasks, and how to tap into other resources.

Each day or more often as needed, refocus on what you have to do, and what you can shed. Here is the way we prioritize things:

1. **Must do.** Things that the law, your boss, your standards, or an emergency require you to do. You may not like them, you may rather do other things, but there's no avoiding these, so best do or delegate them as quickly and as clearly as possible.

2. **Should do.** Your core job. The missions you're on, that take planning and diligence, and that your performance will be judged on—by you, your family, your boss, or your partners. Plan your days and weeks around these.

3. **Nice to do.** These would definitely be worthwhile in the perfect world, but not at the expense of your core job. Things that contribute to the plans of others, to your learning, to your relationships. Do them by all means, but in gaps that emerge in your core program. The 'nice to do's' are a real trap because on their own they seem worthwhile, but together they're a procrastinator's Christmas. Use them to keep your activity menu fresh, not as the whole menu.

4. **Good to do.** Anything else. Often, though, you'll be called in to do something by or for someone else. If it were up to you, the task wouldn't fall into any of the above, yet someone is insistent and it really would help them out. If that's the case, and it is more than a quick fly swat, check with your leader to see what 51 percent call they make, or ask your wingman to take it over—and you'll owe him or her one!

Compare these priorities with your own time management approach and see what approach or combination would suit you best.

Checklists

Of all the things in this book you'll read about, two things stand out as commonplace in the air force, and rare as hen's teeth in our personal and business lives: the debrief and the checklist. Of the two, the checklist is like the poor cousin at the ball. Everyone we talk to gets excited about a nameless, rankless debrief, with all the impact on learning and culture it can carry. Very, very few people get excited about a checklist.

So let us explain why we get excited about a checklist. Using a checklist means we're getting ready to fly. Far from being a poor cousin, our checklists are our wise elders. Working through a pre-flight checklist calms our nerves and puts us on the same frequency as our crew, our team, and our commander. Picking up an emergency checklist gives us time to think and to respond. We know from our checklist that all the basics are in order, so that our mind can drill down to the complexities of our mission and the creativity we'll need to solve its problems.

If we could write another book, it would be 'Checklists are not for Dummies'. Three examples come to mind. One of our pilots flew without his book of checklists just twice in his 30-year military career. Both times, nothing went wrong, there were no emergencies, no accidents. There was no cause for him to look up a checklist, and if he did he probably knew it by heart anyway. But our pilot could not do what he set out to do. Totally missed the mission's objective. Why? Not having his checklists totally derailed his performance. He felt task saturated the whole flight—just a perception that all was not in order.

He's no dummy, and nor are the surgeons at the hospitals who were introduced to checklists for a 2008 study by Harvard public health professor Atul Gawande and his team. The researchers had a hypothesis that simple checklists might help reduce avoidable deaths and complications. But nobody expected by how much. After excluding other factors, they found that deaths occurred in 0.8 percent of operations that used checklists, against 1.5 percent of operations that didn't—a 47 percent reduction. Literally hundreds of lives were being saved. They also found that serious complications fell from 11 percent to 7 percent of operations—a 37 percent improvement. Needless to say, checklists are now mandatory for surgery in those and many other hospitals. Professor Gawande was so astounded he wrote a book, not on public health but called *The Checklist Manifesto*.

Finally, let's go back to the movies. *Apollo 13* captured the moment when aviator Jim Lovell found himself in command of a spacecraft 200,000 miles (321,800 kilometers) from earth, with barely enough battery power to light a torch. NASA was looking at its greatest disaster, and the end of its space program less than a year after the 1969 moon landing. Flight director Gene Kranz, he of 'Failure is not an option' fame, helped keep Lovell and his crew calm, while trying to solve the problem. Ken Mattingly, the astronaut originally slated to fly the mission, was put into a simulator to work out how to fire up *Apollo 13* on a AAA battery. He worked for hours in a race against time, trying sequence after sequence, failing again and again. With everything in the simulated spacecraft turned off and next to no time left, he finally got there. The sequence was transcribed into a simple, step-by-step checklist, and sent to Lovell. It saved Lovell and his crew, the mission, and the NASA space program.

The *Apollo 13* landing proved once again that a checklist beats task saturation under stress. Simplicity beats complexity. Checklists get you home. They have been standard for flying planes since 1935, when a prototype Boeing B-17 Flying Fortress crashed at Ohio's Wright Field due to a stunningly simple pilot error. After take-off, the plane's nose just kept angling up—it didn't level off at all—and eventually the plane was almost vertical, stalled, and dropped back to earth. The air force's best test pilots had just forgotten to unlock the plane's elevator controls—one switch in a hundred steps.

The military realized that even their best people would make mistakes when confronted with the forest of procedures and instruments needed to fly a modern warplane. Checklists have been mandatory ever since. With them, young and inexperienced people can operate rare, expensive machinery in complex situations. Without them, mistakes are certain.

Using three types of checklists

There are three types of checklists you will call upon through your mission—normal, emergency, and reference. Each is just one page, but is different in format and use as follows:

1. **Normal** checklists are condensed memory-joggers of standard operating procedures, so assume that your team knows those procedures. They will also be used in the mission if that procedure is used in the mission. A pilot before take-off will talk his- or herself through the checklist, step by step, to make sure and to ease nerves. That's the sort of checklist you'd want to use before a presentation, or a product launch. Often, the actions can be confirmed to a wingman. In a two-person Do–Confirm: one person does the action, another person verbally confirms it's been done. Not in a narky insistent way, but because it's the natural way the team operates to add confidence and clarity. Do–Confirm, and initial the confirm.

2. **Emergency** checklists, as the name implies, are there at the ready if the team needs them, in a handy case or folder for that purpose. Ideally, the team knows what these procedures are, but it's not necessary—what they have to be able to do is recognize when the checklist is needed, and where to find it. Usually the checklist is in a Read–Do format, for either one or two people. Read the step, do the step, then initial its completion.

3. References are just that: a source of more detailed information you can refer to when you need to. They are comprehensive stores of standard operating procedures, and can be as long as they need to be (and no longer).

Note that these checklists are standard operating procedures: meaning they don't have to be mentioned in the brief, it's assumed that the team will use them. Would that assumption be true of your team? How much work would you have to do to make checklists the norm? Factor in quite a bit: to get buy-in and follow-through—all the things that a change in culture and behavior might need.

Rules for all checklists

There are two critical rules for a checklist: keep it simple, and use it.

The best way to ensure a checklist is simple and used, is for the people who use it to be the ones who write it. Say you've got a team who has done more than their share of product launches and launch events, but there's been a few simple errors of late and you want them to consider a checklist. Or perhaps you've got teams of experienced, frontline operators working on shale oil fracking, offshore wells, coal mine draglines, geoseismic testing. If you rock up one day to any of these teams with a nice sheet of laminated paper and say, 'Hey guys, could you follow this checklist from now on', would they take any notice? It would be much better if you explained that checklists were proven to save lives, time and money, and that it was up to them to create the checklists that worked for them. That's how the best checklists are created, and why they are used. Get specialist help by all means, but don't just deliver the end result.

Failures in offshore drilling have received a lot of warranted publicity in the last decade. Failures on land are more common, if less damaging. In the same period, one international energy company tested the blowout preventers on its active drill pipes every two weeks. Until one day one of the company's best drill operators accidentally sheared the pipe during the test.[2] On investigation, the company found the operator had survived 38 close calls in fewer than a hundred previous tests. The tests were routine, and also dangerous. The operators just didn't focus. After implementing checklists, their focus has returned, and there have been no incidents or close calls since.

Rules for checklists

- **Trigger points** that clearly determine when they are used.
- **One page.** These are memory-joggers, not phone books.
- **Nine steps or less**, including cross-checks. Your team through their standard operating procedures will know what, if anything, makes those possible. There's no need for 'breathing steps', as in 'Remember to breathe', that state the obvious.
- **Clear, concise language**. Really push the meaning-to-ink ratio. If you don't need a word, cut it. If it's not clear to the operator what it means, replace it.
- **No distractions**. Only what has meaning, and no more. Basic fonts, no borders, no decorations, no emojis, no arrows to large words saying 'This is important. Please read', no such large words.
- **Test with other operators**. Not only the team that developed the checklist, but others. They're the ones who will use them, and who will know if they'll work.
- **Keep with the operation**. If it's a checkout checklist, keep it at the checkout. If it's a pipe-testing checklist, keep it with the pipe. If it's a perforation gun, keep it with the gun.

- **Read them aloud**. The checklists are designed for an operator and wingman, whatever the task. Steps, cross-checks, and confirmations are always verbal, and if possible also visual.
- We don't like checklists. They can be painstaking. They're not much fun. But we don't think the issue here is laziness. There's something deeper, more visceral going on. It somehow feels beneath us to use a checklist, an embarrassment. It runs counter to deeply held beliefs about how the truly great among us—those we aspire to be—handle situations of high stakes and complexity. The truly great are daring. They improvise. They do not have protocols and checklists. Maybe our idea of heroism needs updating.

Atul Gawande, *The Checklist Manifesto: How to get things right*[3]

X-GAPS AND EXECUTION RHYTHM (KEEPING THE PLAN TO REALITY)

You'll remember the pilots' mantra: 'Brief the plan, fly the brief.' The brief is the mission; the mission is the brief. Pilots want to feel that their mission has run like a well-scripted, well-rehearsed play: with great timing from every actor, stagehand, and musician; no missed lines; quick recovery from any left-field glitches; each participant having an irresistible energy for getting the job done and done well. If at the end of a mission a pilot can say 'It went according to plan', it's a happy day. It's also a rare one, for plans rarely survive contact with reality. The reasons are infinite, but logically, it's because: the plan was not so good in the first place; someone didn't know the plan; someone hasn't followed the plan; or reality has dramatically changed. Follow Flex to plan–brief– execute–debrief and you'll address the first three of these risks in turn. In this chapter, we'll discuss how to keep the Flex plan wedded to reality—a pretty handy thing in the boardroom, the showroom, the storeroom, or the war room. Plans have to be adapted because the reality of a situation changes. If you know how reality will change, you're smarter and perhaps more divine than most and your plan will reflect that. (In fact, many changes you will have foreseen, and included in the contingencies of your flexible plan.) But if you're human, Flex may help.

Flex accepts that as reality changes, the plan changes. Is that a bad thing? It almost echoes John Maynard Keynes: 'When my information changes, I alter my conclusions. What do you do, sir?'[1] If a sinkhole opens up in the road in front of you, do you drive on regardless? Let's go back to the philosophy behind Flex. It's aiming for flawless execution, not flawless planning. You don't have to obsess about the plan being perfect, because it's the execution that matters. However fast or good your planning, a plan is accurate only for the minute it's made. It will keep changing until captured in the moment of time that is the brief, and then it will continue to change.

So, how do we keep our plan to reality? As we've seen in Chapter 6, 'Flex planning', every Flex plan includes team check-in points, an execution rhythm of regular X-Gap reviews to analyze *the gap between the plan and its execution*. Each X-Gap (short for 'execution gaps') is a decision point for the mission: continue, adjust, or abort? Green light, yellow, or red? If reality changes between X-Gaps, your plan will change too.

This chapter confirms why we need these X-Gaps, when to set them, and how to hold them.

WHY HAVE X-GAP MEETINGS?

Keeping on top of what's happening is the driving reason for our X-Gap meetings, but not the only one. People forget things. (There, we said it. It's out there.) People don't always do what they plan to do. (Truth is hard.) People are more likely to do things when they've committed to do so to someone else. People don't like facing people when they haven't met that commitment . . .

You get the picture. There is simply no better way—without going off on vigilante fantasies—to hold people to their part of the plan. As well as keeping things on track, X-Gap meetings hold people accountable. The plan is *who* does *what* and *when*, and nobody can hide if something's not done. Whether it's an honest oversight or a shirked responsibility, the plan will have to change. You'll be able to head off small problems before they snowball and become big ones. You'll also know there's an internal threat that might have to be managed in future plans. Working through those issues builds teamwork and mutual respect.

X-Gap meetings also underscore the leader's intent and desire for the mission. Just as the brief is the moment for a leader to stamp a personality on the mission, an X-Gap is the time to reset that personality. Every emphasis a leader makes and the mood they create in an X-Gap helps build the team's culture. The leader is restating their responsibility for the plan and its delivery.

Boo found plenty of opportunities to reset the plan and take responsibility for it on the journey with Mode to build a seventeen-story hotel using innovative modular construction. The idea and plan seemed sound—as sound as something that's never been done before could be—but it turned out to have a few gaps. Prime among them was the building material. The concept originated in Papua New Guinea, to control building costs in a place with devastating material and labour cost inflation. Mode used steel boxes, fabricated offshore or in a PNG factory, which could be placed like LEGO blocks to build up the structure. The problem came in transferring the technology to Australia, a country where the building codes and fire standards were based on *concrete* construction. Yet the architect, structural engineers, and fabricators at a regular X-Gap could quickly set a plan to find a solution. The ultimate decision? Mode elected to abandon years of research and engaged an Australian builder of smaller prefabricated buildings, and together they designed and built their hotel. It was a tough decision, leaving behind all that technology and investment capital on the shelf, however we still achieved our mission objective: owning and building a great hotel for less cost than traditional building techniques.

'Corner speed'

Nothing makes the point about X-Gaps better than Commander Zed's three-year mission to replace Australia's long-loved fleet of F-111 strike fighters with two-seat F/A-18F Super Hornets, or Rhinos. Buying military hardware is not cheap and never easy. You can well imagine the economics and politics involved in a once-in-a-generation $6-billion order. In this case, the complexities were magnified because the Super Hornets were only *interim* replacements for the F-111s, pending the delayed arrival of swanky new F-35 joint strike fighters. So Zed had to manage a transition from F-111s to Super Hornets, make sure the new jets complemented the existing fleet of F/A-18C Hornets, and then set up the transition to the F-35s. A triple whammy of objectives, each carrying their own set of risks and complexities.

No amount of up-front planning would pull Zed's team safely through this mission. The game changed every week, and the plan had to change with it. Minor hiccups included repeated concerns over the Hornets' electronics and technical capacities, and the defense minister changing almost annually. Major hiccups included a new Australian government reviewing the whole strategy, not convinced that an interim strike fighter was needed at all. Zed's strategy was to keep pressing on at 'corner speed', the speed (at 300 knots or 555 kilometers per hour) all fighter pilots know gives them maximum performance and maneuverability: fast enough to get to the target and complete the mission, and slow enough to stay safe by taking sharp corners on the run.

To meet that challenge, Zed deliberately drew on some outlier personalities from the RAAF's ranks, people who were more than able in their expertize, but found it hard to think and operate inside the box. They set their X-Gaps weekly as a default, but bounced around that mark. The team first set up their own performance metrics for their cross-check dashboard. They weren't exhaustive, but were all linked directly to the delivery milestones they had to keep. They were chosen to help limit internal reporting time to less than 25 percent of all team time, far less than RAAF project averages. They also captured inherent trade-offs in the mission: for example, if one metric showed a lift in the bomb-carrying capacity of the Super Hornet, another might show a drop in air-to-air combat capacity, another a lift in cost, and another a shift in delivery dates. The whole picture of what they were delivering changed weekly. They weren't just marking off a timeline towards an end delivery that no one wanted.

The 300-knot strategy pushed the bias to action hard, and it worked for two reasons. First was the rigor of the X-Gap meetings in testing and adapting the plan as needed. Rather than set an endpoint and stick to it, the X-Gaps allowed Zed's team to make a succession of small yet significant decisions. The second reason was the team's energy in constantly talking with each set of stakeholders, to bring them along with those decisions. With a change of government rising as a real possibility, Zed's team started conversations with the likely future ministers five months before they won the election. All the talking meant constant testing of assumptions and plan adjustments, and also wide appreciation of the progress and issues of the mission. It kept people on side who would normally be taking pot-shots from outside by providing information that built the minister's situational awareness.

The end result? The first RAAF Super Hornet squadron was declared operational in December 2010, on time and below budget, an unprecedented result at a time when other Australian military hardware purchases were causing severe budgetary and political headaches. As well, the RAAF secured options to order the upgraded EA-18G Growler and any upgrade conversion it may want. That meant Australia had a contingency for any delays in the planned F-35 delivery, and delays there certainly were. What the mission ultimately delivered was well beyond what anyone expected or could have foreseen when it began.

SET FREQUENT X-GAPS

Fighter pilot missions are briefed and flown on the same day. That's their execution rhythm, and they stick to that rhythm for as long as their strategy demands. Business missions take longer. If they're longer than a week, don't wait for reality to change to call an X-Gap meeting. Make it a regular event: the markers of your execution rhythm.

The first X-Gap meeting is the moment of truth. Is the team getting the job done? What culture is emerging? So it makes sense for the meeting to be held early in the mission. Set its timing as part of your brief. In most cases, the meeting has to be held within six days. That way, you create the expectation that the plan *will* be on track within that first week, and that it will stay there.

After that, set as fast an execution rhythm as you can without the X-Gaps getting in the way of execution. A lot of the impact of Flex is in shortening the review cycle. We recently worked with a US bank to help them execute the implementation of a new customer relationship management system, set to be a six-month campaign. As usual, the work involved the bank's IT team, working with the software vendor and an independent IT consultant. The mood at the project kick-off was very positive, a lot of good people confident that they'd get the job done. But we were a little concerned when the first check-in point was set for a month into the schedule. The teams went away on their discrete missions, but when we regathered after the month, nothing substantial had been done, and we were already well behind schedule. The execution rhythm had been set too long: it needed to be weekly, so we could get onto things as soon as they were lagging or veering off plan. That same short cycle has been adopted by Agile, Sprint, or Scrum projects for software development: see 'Flex is agile' at the end of this chapter. There used to be monthly cycles, and now they are weekly.

Here's another balance to get right. It's good that the X-Gaps are held at regular intervals through a mission, but not for dates to be set too far in advance. Dan Ariely is another great thinker from the field of behavioral economics—the branch of economics that accepts that people aren't really economically 'rational' after all, and tries to find out why they don't always act in their financial self-interest. In his book *Predictably Irrational*, Ariely writes how regular, firm deadlines usually generate better results than either self-chosen or end-of-project deadlines.[2] That regular tempo helps create a positive habit of expectation and accountability through the project. Over a long mission that tempo may change, but the changes should be as minimal as possible.

X-GAPS ARE BRIEF AND TO THE POINT

Far from being long and glorious, X-Gaps are short and to the point. Just as a brief is not your typical 'right, here we all are then' kick-off meeting, the X-Gap is not your typical 'right, how are we all then' weekly check-up. Some liken them to a fast-paced fitness session with your trainer: short, focussed, and intense. And they also follow the BRIEF pattern.

Preparation
Everyone in the team prepares for the X-Gap. Each person prepares an honest and accurate statement on the status of their part of the plan. They rank each task either a:

- **green**—completed, or on track and on time
- **yellow**—with issues that *may* block the task's completion, or
- **red**—with critical issues that *will* block the task and risk the mission if not resolved.

And, for every issue raised, the team member brings a possible answer, as well as their thoughts on any changes to relevant threats and resources.

The leader prepares for an X-Gap just as they would for a brief. At minimum, they prepare an updated action plan that captures the team's input. But it is also the moment to reinforce the mission's tone and culture. So, like the brief, preparation is everything.

Two x two x two timing

An X-Gap is formal and serious, and focussed only on the plan. The setting should be the same room as you use to brief—clearly set up as a mission room, not the local cafe. The time you need depends on how many tasks in the plan you have to review. Allow for no more than two minutes at the top, two minutes per task review, and two minutes at the end. If a task review goes over two minutes, hold it over to the end, and then continue in an offline meeting if needed.

We're social beasts, so that sort of timing will be seriously threatened. Some in the team will just revel in getting together, all jokes and inquiries about every last child and pet. If the team needs another get-together to celebrate a milestone or birthday, do that apart from the X-Gap and don't allow the X-Gap to be its planning session. Some will return each week to their pet issues, be it world peace or the need for coffee cup recycling. Some will find irresistible rabbit holes on a technical issue that's *really* interesting, worth at least a three-hour bar detour. All of these risks need to be defused, in the team's own way. A $2 fine jar can work wonders.

B-R-I-E-F again

No surprises, the X-Gap repeats the pattern of Flex planning and briefing as follows:

- **Big picture.** Confirm again why we're doing this thing, where it fits in with your organization's HD Destination and strategy. You'll get some resistance for this. We were helping a great software company execute an equally good business improvement plan from the consulting firm. Our insistence that the big picture be covered at *every* X-Gap drove the consultants crazy—one of many such things no doubt. 'Don't do it,' they cried. 'It's boring, even though we wrote it!' No matter, we invested twenty seconds at the beginning of every X-Gap across 140 teams, literally hundreds of meetings. Why? Well, as fighter pilots, that's just what we do. But also because, before we put our foot down, every debrief at the company revealed the same thing: the team didn't know *why* they were doing what they were being asked to do. They knew their immediate objective, but really hadn't bought into why that objective was needed. Don't be shy about how a mission aligns with the firm's HD Destination. Put it on a chart, put the chart on a wall, and bring it to every meeting.
- **Restate** the mission objective and leader's intent. Note that the mission objective *cannot change*. Here is the critical decision. It may be that the mission's original objective is no longer practical or relevant. If not, it's a red light: abort the mission. That means the X-Gap becomes a debrief, on the spot. And, if a new objective is now needed, the Flex engine starts again: with a new plan, and a new brief.
- **Identify** changes in your top threats and resources. Would those changes prompt any adjustments to the plan?
- **Execute**—The two-minute green–yellow–red review of the plan's tasks. Is it done or not? On track or not? At risk or

not? Here the team is looking to resolve uncertainties and break down barriers. Each member might suggest solutions, but it's the leader's role to resolve them. The focus is only on mission outcomes. It's not a performance review for team members—they have to be held individually and privately. The X-Gap is just about the plan. The plan is progressively updated. Any new actions are spliced in, with the same quick thought given to any lessons and resources. Reallocate or assign resources, add or change tasks.

- **Flexibility** is still needed. Confirm that contingencies are in place for uncontrollable threats, and that they would be effective if played out.

Flex is agile

Many readers will want to compare Flex with other fast cycle approaches to performance delivery and improvement, in particular the 'Agile' models for software development, which are undoubtedly effective for their purposes.

The term 'Agile' stems from the 2001 Agile Manifesto of a group that included the creators of Scrum, Extreme Programming (XP), Dynamic Systems Development Method (DSDM), and Crystal. The manifesto sets out four core values for enabling high-performing teams, and Flex embodies all of these values. Interestingly these processes were co-developed by a fighter pilot, Jeff Sutherland, who is now also the CEO of Scrum Inc. He was a graduate of the Top Gun School, flew over 100 missions in Vietnam and to top it off became a doctor at the University of Colorado School of Medicine.

Of these models, Flex and Scrum stand out as the most streamlined. They have a smaller number of core practices, roles, and artifacts that together form a solid base to build from. Other approaches—SAFe, Rage Less DAD, DSDM, and Crystal Clear for example—have a large portfolio of possible practices and roles, from which you pick and choose.

While Flex and Scrum are both powerful approaches for getting things done, they can be used together as they emphasize different aspects of the challenge. Table 5 sets out that comparison. Most importantly, Flex offers tighter alignment with an organization's ultimate objectives, a greater focus on team culture and development, and more ways to keep a team and each individual in it on track. While Scrum and other Agile approaches are effective in completing short-term sprints as part of long-term projects, they are not designed to answer what those sprints and projects should be.

This matters more and more as firms struggle to align their IT efforts with business outcomes and objectives, particularly where they've invested in myriad methods, frameworks, processes, and services. You need something that is simple and intuitive to draw these elements together tightly, align them with business objectives, and respond quickly to external threats and opportunities. Something that sits lightly on the organization, without displacing its existing processes. Users of Flex find that it serves this role well.

Table 5: Comparing Scrum, Kanban and Flex

Element	Scrum*	Kanban*	Flex
Purpose	Deliver quality software	Deliver quality manufacturing	Deliver quality, aligned products and service
Change philosophy	Only before/ after sprint	Any time	Any time, guided by situational awareness
Organizational development	Quality, speedy delivery (QSD)	Quality, speedy delivery (QSD)	Quality, speedy, aligned, informed agility
Team development	Team accountability	Individual accountability	Team and individual accountability
Leader development	Support process	-	Support process and culture
Direction	-	-	High-definition destination
Path	Release, Feature, Theme, Epic	Work in Progress	Strategy and operation
Major effort	Project (>1 month)	-	Campaign (>2 months)
Component effort	Sprint (<1 month)	Continuous flow	Mission (<2 months)
Roles	Product owner, scrum master, team	Supervisor, individuals	Champion, Team leader ACE, team
Owner of effort	Scrum master	-	Team leader

Cont.

Element	Scrum*	Kanban*	Flex
Guidance for effort	Backlog ordered by Product owner	Work in progress limits	Team leader's intent
Objective	Increment in potentially shippable product	Workflow to done state delivering value	Team's mission objective
Prioritization	Product owner value rank in backlog	Product owner value rank in backlog	Champion resolves clashes, finds resources
Scoreboard	Velocity, burn downs, burnups, information radiators	Kanban board	Dashboard
Plan	Refinement and Sprint planning meeting	Pull work (Team Choice)	Six-step planning
Brief	Sprint planning team commits	-	Brief
Execute	Daily scrum meeting, Sprint review	Build	Wingman, task shedding, checklists
Plan revision	Product owner ends Sprint; interrupts pattern	Review and measure	X-Gap
Review	Demo (aka Scrumming the Scrum, aka Retrospective)	-	Debrief, Lessons learned

Source: Table data drawn from multiple sources, including www.atlassian.com/agile.

THE DEBRIEF

For many, the standout feature of the Flex engine is the debrief. That's not only because a debrief is so powerful, but because it is so rare. In business, government, and our personal lives, we finish a job just in time to either pass out or sweep on to the next one. Outside the military, very few teams stop to consider what they've just achieved—win, lose, or draw—and what they and other teams might learn from that effort.

Teams that debrief are not just learning from each mission, but putting that learning into action on their very next mission. Flex teams have always been agile, in the language of today, and pivot at every opportunity. We're talking about short-term missions that are being repeated, driving better execution on every cycle. If similar problems are being experienced across different teams, then your organization can put that part of its operations under a blowtorch, and set new standards.

Yet the debrief is a must not only for your speed of learning, but for your team's culture. The hallmark phrase of the debrief is 'It's not who's right, it's what's right'. Let's go back to how the New York Giants first started their Flex debriefs in 2011, and how debriefs were the common practice of the eleven conference-leading teams in the 2015 season (see Chapter 2, 'What is Flex?'). 'Through the debriefs, the Giants learned from themselves what they had to do if they were going to make the Super Bowl again. They'd taken responsibility for their own performance, as individuals and as a team. They got better each week. The debriefs built in energy and purpose. Each player identified what they had to do better, very specifically, and what help they needed from others to do that.'[1]

For the Giants, 'Eli Manning picked out 30 plays and as the clip of a single play ran, anyone who saw something he felt he could've done better was supposed to speak up. If a player didn't own up to an error, one of his teammates could point it out.'

Only that never happened, receiver Michael Clayton said: 'When a Brandon Jacobs run came on the screen, the running back almost immediately said, "I should've hit that hole harder." On a pass play, a lineman said, "I need to knock that end's hands down so you've got a clearer path to throw, Eli." Receivers said they needed to catch balls and block safeties better. Tight end/fullback Bear Pascoe said only a couple times did Manning maybe add a point or two.'

With that, the Giants went on to win the Super Bowl. You can see that what they were taking on was as much about their culture as about their learning. Positive culture and learning are the two big payoffs of doing debriefs often and well. In helping with debriefs, the lesson we have learned time and again is that communication within the team has been a missing link. If things were being said, others hadn't heard it—that's a learning issue.

More likely, things weren't being said because people weren't comfortable saying it—that's a culture issue. People held things in. They did not want to expose their errors to a supervisor or boss who would all too readily pin blame. They did not want to give a competitor at work any hint of an advantage. They did not want to admit error to another division.

On the A$18.5 billion Gladstone liquefied natural gas plant, for example, construction milestones weren't being met, in large part due to miscommunication and conflicting expectations between critical subcontractors. Both parties were partially responsible for the delays, but discussing them was impossible as each had its defensive shields firmly in place. 'Slash' ran a debrief that, as always, focussed on the facts not the blame. A twenty-minute meeting driven by the right questions was all it took: half the time that the participants had set aside. Digging down they quickly confirmed that the way they shared information did not work for either party. Fixing that was a big step towards a stronger collaborative culture. Free from defensive feelings and able to question what was working and what wasn't, their communication and the project itself went a lot faster and smoother.

These are not isolated examples. In 2012, the Group for Organizational Effectiveness in Albany, New York, reviewed all of the 46 studies on the effects of debriefing in business, medical, aviation and other settings, and drew some strongly favourable conclusions.[2] It found that, on average, 'properly conducted' debriefs improved team and individual performance by 20 to 25 percent. More structured and disciplined debriefs improved performance by a higher 35 to 40 percent, on average. And, importantly, the authors found that debriefs require little time and few material resources.

The debrief we run is called a STEALTH debrief, and it has the elements that the Group for Organizational Effectiveness identifies as essential for an effective debrief: active dialogue rather than passive feedback; aimed at development not evalua-tion; reviewing specific events; from multiple perspectives. The acronym stands for the actions you take: see section 'Practicing STEALTH'. Though it jars a bit to call something 'stealth' in a

Flex approach renowned for its transparency, the name works for us because a well-executed debrief really is your secret weapon. Primary among its secrets is its tone: what we call nameless and rankless, pilots figuratively taking off their name and rank insignia when they enter the room. In the debrief room, hierarchies and egos don't matter; leadership, standards, communication, and knowledge do.

If you think there's too much hierarchy in your organization for a debrief, try the military. If you think there's no time for a debrief, try combat. If you think a debrief won't work in sport or business or even at home, consider the examples given in this chapter. Better still, give it a go with your team. We believe the debrief is the single most powerful tool you can lead with.

'Wise leaders are always engaged in and by the world;
they are open to 'reflective backtalk',
they can admit errors and learn from their mistakes.'

Noel Tichy and Warren Bennis, *Judgment*[3]

LEARNING AND CULTURE

The disciplined military practice of debriefing was conceived and developed by the U.S. Air Force during the Vietnam War. Before then, through World War II and the Korean War, the Air Force debriefed in the same way that other forces did: at the bar with very minimal note-taking. But as we saw in Chapter 1, 'The origins of Flex', the U.S. Navy and Air Force were losing far more planes and pilots than their technological advantage should have allowed. The immediate response was the quick but formal debrief, close to what we know it as now. From then on the debrief would be a ritual practiced with discipline and devotion, because it saved lives. It became a place where everyone who was part of the mission could hash out what went right, what went wrong, what that meant, and what could be done about it. It became open and honest, the nameless, rankless forum that searched for root causes irrespective of who was involved. Frank and sometimes frankly intense, the debrief became a place where everyone, aces and novices, could learn how to survive and complete their mission.

Agility: Fast learning and action

If you debrief your every action, learning and understanding what happened every time, then your learning accelerates. The last time you learned so fast, you were a toddler. Yet the idea is not just to learn from your own fun and adventures, it is to learn from everyone in your organization, past and present. As we will see, one point of the debrief is to flush out what the team learned from their mission. The other point is to capture those lessons learned and share them. These are the lessons that teams consider every time they plan. These lessons are used immediately by the same team on their next mission. They are also codified into standards, and assumed to be known by others in the organization. Either way, they are not filed away to go stale; they live and breathe through each stage of the Flex cycle. From an early age, many of us are encouraged to 'learn by doing'. Yet we don't automatically realize *what* we should learn from each event, and do not have perfect recall of those lessons when we require them. We need to work at these things, and the debrief is just one part of that discipline. (We'll talk about sharing knowledge and standards in Chapter 14, 'The Flex wings'.)

'Lips' saw this accelerated learning when debriefs were introduced at Manheim Car Auctions in 2014. More cars are sold per day at Manheim than anywhere else on earth. The company was founded in Atlanta in 1945, when there were quite a few excess military vehicles to deal with. Now, at their Hayward site in California, Manheim shifts 2300 cars in a morning, each and every week—a dozen stands selling a car every 60 seconds when the whole scene is at full throttle. How did they reach that sort of efficiency? Traditionally, with the boss sharing data and thoughts for a half-hour or so. Normally, that happened at 8 p.m., which seemed a little late. So Lips set a Flex debrief for 6 p.m. the next day. The sales team got there at 6.25 p.m. (better but not at all great), and Lips started through the STEALTH process. Instead of the boss's view, the team got the whole team's view. Every night, a couple of ideas were captured to improve the run of the day. People talked, were listened to, took notes. Imagine not just the first time, but the fifth, the eighth, the tenth. By the end of two weeks, the debriefs had generated enough lessons learned for the day to finish at 6 p.m., when the debriefs now took place. That was quite a change—for the team and their families. And in just that time, an already strong facility did its day's work in two hours less time: they were preparing and moving cars more quickly, in the right order, with less reworking.[4]

If that sort of learning is possible at one facility, what would happen if the lessons were shared across a company? Medtronic is one of the world's largest medical technology and services companies, founded in 1949 in Minneapolis and now headquartered in Dublin, Ireland, with over 85,000 employees globally. It works on non-pharmaceutical solutions for cardiac and vascular, neurological and spinal, diabetes, orthopaedics, and other common, sometimes life-threatening, conditions. Many of its solutions are innovative, so they have to be tried within a trusted doctor–patient relationship if they are to be adopted. If a doctor will trial a therapy, there is a strong chance the patient will be pleased with the results. The hard part is getting that trial.

At Medtronics, 'Lips' worked with the national sales division, responsible for one set of medical solutions. Its sales president had nine teams reporting to him through nine sales vice presidents.

The issue was that the VPs saw themselves more in competition than as a single team, working in regional silos without sharing what they were learning. The sales president had a weekly call with each VP to review how they were going. The VPs only felt good about the call if they were ahead of their targets, which like every business was often but not always, and they also wanted to get out and meet those targets rather than talk about them. So the sales president took a different tack. Instead of nine calls, he made one. Instead of reviewing individual results, he reviewed what the teams were doing. He structured the calls as a debrief, and pushed for cause and effect—the results were noted, but really irrelevant. In the first week, the Washington VP shared how his team had started a new conversation with a medical center. The Florida VP followed that lead and shared how her team had worked around a problem a doctor had with another device. The ideas started flowing. Each and every week they debriefed in the same objective way, full of curiosity rather than fear. Within four months, the division had sold out of its product. The VPs couldn't get enough of these calls. They were learning almost too fast.[5]

Tight culture

It's always hard and often dangerous to try and describe the culture that you want in your team. A small dictionary of adjectives has been used: honest, open, performance, excellence, trusting, reliable, disciplined and more. If there's one word we'd use, it would be 'tight'. A team that is tight will be there for each other. It will perform purposefully and efficiently, in a way that honesty and humanity allows. Its people will fit together snugly, both in their roles and personalities, to bring the richest skillset and awareness to the team and its job. They will trust and respect each other. Their leader will have uncontested responsibilities. It's a tight team.

The debrief is a must for a tight team. The author Jim Collins, who we will consider again shortly, believes that truth within an organization is essential for a successful organization, and that some form of debrief is essential for that truth. 'When you conduct autopsies without blame, you go a long way toward creating a climate where the truth is heard.'[6] (That term 'autopsy' presumes a death: a little ghoulish for our liking, and ignores that our wins are debriefed just the same as our losses.) The 'T' in STEALTH is for the Tone of the debrief: the climate in which learning, leadership, openness and honesty can thrive to meld a tight team. Again, Flex is not just a mechanical process, but the culture and climate in which it takes place. Peter Senge observes that when organizations try to copy a military-style debrief, they do it in a sterile way, just going through the motions without living the learning opportunity, without sharing the lessons learned.[7]

The debrief nurtures and motivates a tight team in many quite different ways. Here it's worth considering who is in your team. If your team is full of rock-star professionals, highly skilled and highly motivated, you may find little need for team talks to get things going. Yet still a clean debrief is needed for each mission. On the other hand, if your team is just starting out, a bit nervous or made up of average Joes, then a debrief offers essential psychological and learning support for them to quickly get on top of their roles.

First, the debrief gives the team closure on its accomplishment, closes the loop on their experience. Whatever has happened, there may be feelings from the mission that you don't want to carry over to the next. There may be too much pride in the accomplishment, or little annoyances or frustrations between team members. Good or bad, don't let those feelings linger. Recognize the mission for what it was, acknowledge it, and move on.

Second, acknowledging the quick wins of a mission is critical for a longer term mission. It's the need, as John Kotter calls it, to generate short-term wins.[8] Debriefing reinforces that there have been wins. It helps gain momentum and confidence. Teams understand that it's not a lucky streak, that they are building their ability to lead, to change, to get things done—even on a long, complex and uncertain mission. A team that has had a month of short-term wins and learned from each one in a debrief is feeling pretty good about itself and the changes it's made. So too each individual on that team.

Third, win or lose, the debrief reinforces the team's ownership of the result. It is not about individual performance, but team performance. Just as there is no blame being cast, the debrief is not a claim for personal credit. As we'll see, its focus is on what happened, not who is responsible. Good or bad, the team learns from what worked and what didn't, from what its individuals did well or otherwise. Each person gets to understand and respect the challenges and successes that their comrades have met and achieved. Each person gets to appreciate the honesty with which their comrades talk about what they might have done better. Each person takes on the responsibility to learn from what they hear.

Finally, the debrief builds the leadership needed for a tight team. Just like every other part of Flex, we believe leadership can be learned from sound principles and the opportunities to practice them. Debriefs are one of those opportunities. Leadership is developed, practiced, displayed, and observed. At a debrief, everyone works through the same pattern, starting with the team leader: examining what happened and what they could do better individually, and how to capture that learning for next time. Junior executives have the opportunity to follow the modelling of their mentors. The next wave of corporate or family leaders are being formed.

But enough already. Let's see when and how to do a STEALTH debrief.

WHEN TO DEBRIEF

Here's the trick: debrief *every* mission—big or small; win, lose, or draw—*immediately* you've finished executing it. They're two hard disciplines to accept, but they're the only way to capture the benefits of the debrief. No matter how small the mission, for any action that has a discrete result, do the debrief. Whatever the result of the mission, no matter how tired you are, no matter how urgent the next thing is, do the debrief. Your mission isn't over until you do, just like the Flex engine says: plan–brief–execute–debrief.

Debrief win, lose, or draw

Many people resist a debrief because they misunderstand what it is. They fear it's to go over the coals of failure, and assign blame and punishment. That misunderstanding disappears through the habit of debriefing *everything*. Whatever the result of the mission, debrief it. Success, failure, near misses, close calls—all of them are the product of your work and a bit of luck. Imagine if you debriefed only your failures and near misses. How depressing would that be! Enjoy the successes as well, but note that you can always do better, and might have just been lucky!

Near misses or close calls are those times when the mission met its objective, but it was perhaps lucky to do so. These are particularly valuable to debrief, as they take place free from the consequences of failure. That's clean air to work in, and a good opportunity for learning. People can talk about what went off track, and how the team recovered from that. For airlines, near misses are reviewed as critical incidents, so serious is what might have been. The Children's Hospital of Minneapolis had the idea of using 'good catch logs', for nurses to anonymously log when they discovered something not quite right with a patient's treatment, and for those logs to be studied independently by others not directly concerned with the treatment.[9] That was an effective practice to improve the safety record of the hospital, but the learning took time, and lacked personal accountability.

For similar reasons, wins are a must to debrief. The idea is to tease out what was good planning and execution, and what was plain good luck. It's also the moment to review and rebuild situational awareness to consider whether the same actions would deliver the same results in the future. The author Jim Collins had to conduct his own debrief after many of the companies lauded as business stars in his book *Good to Great* soon became financial black holes.[10] One of them was Circuit City: number two electronics retailer in the U.S. in 1998, bankrupt in 2008. Another was Fannie Mae, a giant mortgage lender at the center of the 2007 financial crisis. Collins studied these and other black holes to consider how their cultures may have held clues to their downfall that their annual reports did not. In *How the Mighty Fall*, he concluded that the first stage of that fall was that those companies had silenced the truth within.[11] They believed their own press. They never questioned their own actions. They never debriefed their success to consider *why* they were winning, and if those root causes were sustainable. In the end, they were not.

Debrief the moment after you execute, as part of the mission

The debrief is an integral part of the mission itself, not something that happens afterwards. Don't make it a big deal at the end of a large and long campaign, do it quick and dirty at the end of each short mission. Fighter pilots get out of their jets, drop off their helmets and flight gear, and go direct to the debrief room, every time. The Blue Angels debrief the same routine, over 250 times a year, and still discover new things. They're not the only ones. The U.S. Marines call their debriefs After Action Reports (AARs). Shawn served as an embedded journalist during the 2003 Iraq War, being part of Marine units at the frontline for two-week missions, returning each time to write up the experience. Each time, before the unit could even shower after a fortnight in the field, they completed their AAR, sharing their thoughts with note-taking officers, who would immediately include any useful intelligence in the briefs for the outgoing units.

That level of learning is immediate and continuous. Is it possible in your team? It can be. Factor in the time. Treat the debrief seriously. At the end of every team mission there's a heap of housekeeping to do: filing receipts, boxing up papers, celebrating the result, reporting back to stakeholders. All of that takes longer than a debrief. Debrief the same day your execution phase ends or the next business day, not the next week. Remember, it can be as short as five minutes and never more than an hour—however long it takes to identify two or three lessons learned, maximum. That mission is just on one part of your journey, not the whole trip. But the mission isn't over until the debrief is over.

PRACTICING STEALTH

A Flex debrief is not an open session to shell peas and pistachios and ponder the team's fortunes. Just like a Flex plan or briefing session, there is a discipline to running a debrief, in a way that works. To do so is to run through the following steps:

- **Set up.** Prepare the time, the place, the people, the materials, yourself.
- **Tone.** Nameless, rankless, starting with the leader's own mistakes.
- **Execution against objective.** Flex objectives are measurable. Did you meet them?
- **Analysis of execution.** How and why did we succeed or fail?
- **Lessons learned.** What clear lessons did we learn from this mission?

- **Transfer of lessons.** Who needs this lesson, how fast, and how will we get it to them?
- **High note.** End the debrief, and the mission, with a positive sense of accomplishment.

These are the steps that every debrief has to go through. They may not take long or include much ceremony, but they have to be there. For each one, we'll offer the basic information in bullet points, and only explain them when we have to.

Set up

This is not just the time and place, but who will be there and what they will need as follows:

- **When.** As we've seen, this is after your course of action has been completed, and before the mission ends. Set specific times for the start and end, no more than one hour. Set specific times or build timing expectations for each step in between. This is a time to listen and learn, not to dwell. Finish on time, to the minute. That's effective leadership and builds your credibility. If you can't finish a simple debrief on time, how are you going to go with complex project deadlines.
- **Where.** The debrief space should be the same mission room that you used for the briefing or, if you have the space, a room set aside just for debriefing. It should not be an everyday work or meeting room. It needs to be a sanctuary in which the team feels psychologically safe. Ensure the room is clean; no dirty whiteboards, lunchtime scraps or coffee cup stains. Check the whiteboard markers aren't dry or permanent.
- **Who.** This is reserved only for the mission team itself, and it must include them all. Unlike a planning session, there is no need for external experts, and certainly no room for other teams or people up or down the hierarchy. Others will share

in the lessons learned and the standard reports. This is team business.

Here's where the team's diversity pays off again. Just as mission planning benefits from your diverse skills and perspectives, the debrief will draw out different interpretations of the same event. Different people are sensitive to different things, their situational awareness making them alert to different risks. By themselves, they can hold and describe different parts of the mission 'elephant'. Only when they share their perspective can the team see the whole elephant—a richer appreciation of just what went on in the mission. Only when surgical teams take on the views of everyone in the room—surgeons, anaesthetists, scrub techs, circulating techs, nurses—can they get a clear and objective view of what was going on.

Make sure the team covers certain roles. The mission leader (who may not be the most senior person) leads the debrief. Assign a timekeeper, a scribe, and someone who will disseminate any data or lessons learned from the debrief.

- **What.** Have available at the debrief any data you need to review performance against objectives. This includes what we call 'debrief focus points', that is, notes that the team has taken throughout the mission on what may be useful to debrief at its end. If something bad has happened, or there's been a near miss, or something saved a near miss, or an unusually good achievement—all things that should be noted and included in the debrief, as these are the things likely to lead to lessons learned.

  If it was a complex mission or course of action, make sure you've got the room ready with plenty of whiteboards or flipchart paper. Pages are needed to present or capture a timeline of action, the mission plan and objective, execution versus objectives, the successes and errors, their causes and lessons learned, and the traditional 'parking lot' for ideas that might need to be actioned later.

- **How.** Debriefs have the obvious meeting rules of mutual respect: no phones, no interruptions. Beyond that, we go to the next steps.

Tone

What does it take for everyone in the team to feel absolutely comfortable about discussing their role in the mission's success or failure? That is a massive achievement for most teams, and it doesn't come by accident. People need to feel safe and respected to reach that point. Getting the tone right, from the start of the debrief, is at the core of its value. The debrief is the true marker of the team's culture, and the strongest tool for making and keeping it tight. As such, the team leader's role is critical. You need an open and honest mind, and the willingness to admit mistakes. You have to set both the ground rules and the example as follows:

- **Nameless and rankless.** This is not a gimmick, but one of the two actions that most set a debrief's tone. The point about a debrief being 'nameless, rankless' is that *everyone* in the team is just an actor in the mission's play. You lose your name, your title, even your personality. Fighter pilots refer to their *roles* in the team rather than their names or nicknames. They were the squadron 'leader' or number two or three or four on the mission, and so they are in the debrief. Do anything you can do to remove your persona from the room, and replace it with a detached, objective viewer of the mission.
- **An open mind for open listening.** It is not at all rare for two people on a team to be in the same conversation but 'hear' different words spoken. What happens is that one person is expecting to hear something, and so hears it regardless of

whether it is actually said or not. Scientists call it 'predictive perceptual signaling'. More often than not it's a very useful human trait for filling gaps in what we see or hear. But we make mistakes. We think we know what's coming, or we think we know the answer, so our minds literally stop listening, and move on to their own conclusions. You need a conscious effort to stop listening for what you expect to hear. The debrief is the perfect place to practice.

- **Leader owns up first.** Nothing will encourage the team more to honesty than you calling out what you could have done better. It may often be said that 'It's not a weakness to make mistakes; it's a weakness to hide them.' But people need to feel safe. When it comes to the crunch of finding out what happened (A=Analysis), any mistake will be uncovered. Owning up to one's mistake puts one in a better position than someone else pointing it out, and far better than not even being aware of it. A leader who starts with that truthful self-criticism is demonstrating the courage and integrity you want in your team. Even if your performance was really pretty good, find something to raise that you could have done better. Then open the discussion to others: 'Did anyone else see me do anything dumb, different or dangerous?' Demonstrate that the debrief is nothing to do with blame or discipline, but only about finding out what happened and why. Expose yourself for the team to be stronger.

- **A closed circle.** The clear rule is that what is said in the debrief stays in the debrief. The team itself decides what lessons learned and what tacit knowledge leaves the debrief room. The only things mentioned at the debrief are those things immediately relevant to the mission's performance. They will have no relevance to anyone outside the room, unless the team itself decides so. Only then will the debrief underpin the sanctity of performance and the team's eagerness to learn.

Execution against objective

Often, we're asked to check in on how a team is performing. It may be on the execution of a corporate strategy, or just a recently completed event. With all the best intent in the world, this step is where the debrief ends. What was the objective and the course of action to get there? Oh, can't really say? OK, let's not worry about last time, and start talking about next time . . .

If you've been working with Flex to this point, though, this is perhaps the most straightforward part of the debrief. You'll have a mission objective that is measurable. Did the team reach it: yes or no? What were the hits and misses? What were the debrief focus points?

You'll have been tracking your course of action through your X-Gap meetings. Was each step completed: yes or no? Take them one step at a time, just as they're laid out in the planned course of action. Analyze them one step at a time (see below). Build up the picture of what happened and why. Don't assume you know why things have happened the way they have. Just let the process take its course, and your team's perspectives be shared.

These are the results of the mission, in black and white. Then, consider whether to go a little further and test the *effects* of the mission. Say the team met its objectives. Say it executed its course of action all but flawlessly. Yet did those actions have the effect that the leader and the organization intended and would want? Remember the ball bearing factories of Schweinfurt? A brilliantly executed mission, that achieved next to no valuable effects. That's what the team needs to consider.

Analysis of execution

This steps takes us from knowing what happened, to knowing how and why it happened. The team takes the first result and asks 'How did this happen?' and, for each statement in response,

'Why?' The answers may or may not be obvious. Keep drilling down: *why, why, why.* You will get to a root cause, the first action or inaction that led to what happened. You may also come to realize there is no such thing as a single cause, since everything that happens is a result of a chain of events, and any link in that chain would have changed the course of events. But the root cause is the first in that chain. It may not have been the sweetest action or the worst mistake, but it was the first.

To guide the analysis, we can go back to the Flex framework for action, to help isolate the different factors that may have contributed to the end results. Table 6 sets out those possible factors. It's a useful checklist to run an eye over to make sure you've got to the causes you need to. Consider both successes and misses. If the mission met its objective, but had a different effect than intended, what let you down: the planning, situational awareness through the mission, the strategy itself? If you made it through a near miss, was it experience that got you through? Did you need that experience to overcome a situation that the plan might have foreseen? Is the lesson learned to plan

Table 6: Potential causes and root causes of success or failure

Core	Team	Plan	Execute
HD Destination	Leadership	Objective	People to plan:
Alignment	Organization	Threat	-Task saturation
Strategy	Communication	Resources	-Cross-checks
Training	Knowledge	Lessons learned	-Mutual support
Standards	Experience	Course of action	Plan to reality: -Situational awareness
	Discipline	Contingencies	-X-Gap

for that situation, or to keep the plan flexible and rely on the experience?

Finally, make the whole process visual and you'll find another benefit. At each debrief, put the four headings below on a flipchart or screen, and capture the root causes that have led to mistakes or to surprising successes. Then, through a longer-term campaign, line up those mission debriefs and see what is common. If a communication or an alignment issue comes up repeatedly—teams pushing hard but in the end in a different direction to what the leader intended—then you've identified the need for new standards in those areas.

Working through the results, you'll now have a fair idea of what happened and why. It will be apparent what was done well, and what was done not so well. This is the moment to take team and individual ownership for that performance, starting with the team leader. This is where the team leader steps up and says, 'I made these mistakes, and I'm going to fix them.' That's how the flight leaders for the U.S. Navy's Blue Angels start off. It releases tension for the team, and demonstrates that it's OK to make a mistake, as long as you learn from it. And that's the whole point of the debrief.

Lessons learned

If you're moderately self-aware and a little bit curious, it's pretty hard to think of a single action you take that doesn't offer a lesson learned. The longer we live and stay open-minded, the more those lessons mount up. Yet the debrief isn't the place to volunteer every personal breakthrough. What we're looking for is something prominent, a root cause or pattern that will re-occur. Managing that in a different way can be a pivot to stronger future performance, by becoming a *standard* for your organization and your team, something that can be replicated by others, safely and reliably. For example, in exercise debriefs in different conditions,

Boo's squadron regularly reviewed the three-dimensional distances that their jets could be incoming towards each other before they had to veer course to avoid a collision, yet close enough to be in a position to outmaneuver the other aircraft. The lesson learned needs to be explicit and actionable, effective in improving speed, quality, or safety next time someone tries a similar mission. These lessons are hard lessons, usually developed as a result of an incident where lives are nearly, or actually, lost.

That's not easy to do, so don't be surprised if there are *no* lessons learned in your debrief. For many of our pilots and facilitators, drawing out actionable lessons learned from a debrief is the hardest part of Flex. That makes a kind of sense: lessons are valuable, so they don't come easy. Keep pushing though for the few minutes allotted. One single lesson learned is better than none.

Transfer of lessons

If this step sounds like filing a note in your firm's database, then we haven't done a good job in explaining it yet. How do you transfer the lessons? Like everything else in Flex, there are no set answers, only questions. The questions here are as follows:

- Who needs this information?
- How fast do they need it?
- So, how will we get it to them?

How you get a lesson into the minds of those who need it most will vary from an urgent call to a team already in action, to creating a checklist that captures the new standard operating procedure. Anything in between might touch on the organization's formal communication and knowledge structures. That means making sure your lesson is in the right system, and is searchable. But don't wait for your knowledge management or internal communications team to make a fuss about the news. Share the lesson with anyone you think might appreciate the thought, or appreciate that you are keeping in touch with them. If the lesson is important enough to change your standard operating procedures, it's *interesting* to the right people. Let them know!

High note

Whatever happened to the mission, whatever happened in the debrief, finish on a positive note. Remember, just doing the debrief is time well spent. The team has committed itself to learn from its actions, and to share those lessons with those who should know. That's no small feat in most organizations. Sometimes, the effort of completing a mission will leave people exhausted and flat. Sometimes, when there's no debrief, the team just seems to dissolve and move onto the next job, without ceremony or acknowledgement. That will never happen with a debrief. The end of the brief will always be more positive than the end of the mission itself. There will *always* be positives to draw out of the mission, or the brief, or both. Single one out to finish the formal debrief process, and give personal thanks for the effort your team put into the mission, and the honesty you all put into the debrief. Don't go back and summarize the results, or anything at all. The team has all it needs now. End it well.

JUST DEBRIEF

We've heard every excuse in the book for not running a debrief. Time is the big one. In most organizations, we're told, 'There is simply no time to spare for this type of navel gazing. We have to get on to the next thing, and we're already a week behind. We don't get the team together even to celebrate a win, let alone trawl through the ashes of a failure.' Yet why are you already a week behind? You don't want to debrief how you got to that?

Every organization that has made the debrief part of its culture has had the same experience. The lessons and culture gained from them far outweigh the modest time spent. There is always time for a debrief. You will rarely get a better return on an investment of time. Time is really the excuse. What truly stops a debrief is fear and ego. A debrief calls on a team to be honest with each other, and calls on a leader to acknowledge their mistakes. Depending on the individuals and the culture, that may not be easy.

Working patiently through the clear, simple, proven structure of a debrief is the best way we know to overcome these barriers. The first time may well be awkward, like all first times. You're new to this and so is your team. But stick to your guns, and see it through. We guarantee it will be worth it. Before long, the phrase 'Let's debrief' will be met with as much appreciation as 'What are you having?' Just debrief.

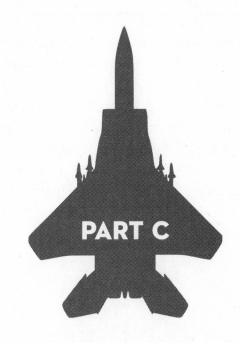

PART C

THE FLEX COCKPIT
AND WINGS

In the Flex cockpit, two things come together. The pilot has to think the same way whether they are a team leader or a follower who may soon be called on to lead. You have to be aware of your situation, know everything about the mission plan, and about your team and how it will execute that plan. In a larger organization, the cockpit is also the place where the pilot's thinking aligns with their organizational thinking. Each team member has to have a very sharp idea of the organizational purpose and strategy, and how their own mission and *their own role in that mission* will fulfill that purpose. Meanwhile, the Flex wings are giving each team member the skills, standards and confidence they need to rely on each other and fulfill their mission.

That's a lot going on. Fortunately, the Flex engine of plan–brief–execute–debrief is an extremely effective way to harness all of that energy, thinking, and action. Let's build up how that works.

12

SITUATIONAL AWARENESS

Flex is not about pure efficiency and commitment to task, come what may. If your team doesn't know what its threats are, or doesn't know the effects of its actions, it won't survive. You're what we call 'tumbleweed'—just blowing in the wind. Instead, if your team wants to operate successfully within a system, it needs to know its place in that system. It needs to have situational awareness or, in fighter pilot speak, 'SA'.

Remember the story of Lance Corporal Cabezas and his unit, coming across a village farmer in Afghanistan? The strategy called for winning the hearts and minds of the local Afghans, not simply keeping Allied soldiers safe. If that was the strategy, there was precious little guidance on how it should be achieved. It relied on each unit's awareness of their operating environment, and how to engage with the locals in it. Cabezas had the situational awareness to appreciate that this chance meeting was a great opportunity. If Cabezas was unaware of that situation, he would not have engaged with the villager, let alone help him dig a ditch. A chance meeting led him to make the most of the opportunity.

Fighter pilots have a very particular understanding of what situational awareness is. The situation is the airspace above and the ground below within their field of action, which is a pretty large area when you're cruising for, say, two hours at 600 miles (966 kilometers) per hour. To have situational awareness within that field is to know who is trying to do what, who is moving where, as well as the status of your jet, your squadron, and your mission. In other words, everything you might come in contact with or have to make a decision about over that 1000-mile stretch.

Put simply, situational awareness is knowing what's going on around you. That includes the dimension of time: situational awareness is four-dimensional. You have an appreciation of why things are as they are, and what they may be in the future. Looking back, you understand the operating environment or system you're in, the mission you're on, and your plans for that mission. Looking around, you understand what everyone is doing in that environment, friend and foe, and the resources they can draw on. Looking forward, you understand the effects of your actions, and the threats to your mission. You are aware of what is and what might be.

In this chapter we look at the two main types of situational awareness that Flex draws on. The first is the line-of-sight alignment to your mission objective: understanding the effects of everything you and the impact that has on your objective. The second is a simple approach to systems thinking: an appreciation that you are always working within a system, and anything you do will have an effect on that system.

We also talk about how to build situational awareness. Though an emerging leader will become known for his or her situational awareness, it is most importantly a team quality. Team diversity matters. Team consciousness matters. This sounds hard. But teams can build awareness skills just as they can build their execution skills. Building situational awareness is simply part of Flex.

LINE-OF-SIGHT ALIGNMENT

One of the most critical elements of situational awareness is the ability to see the *effects* of your actions all the way up to your organizational High-definition (HD) Destination. That means tracing your actions to how they lead to your mission objective, to how that objective meets your leader's intent, to how that intent is part of your organization's strategy and performance, and how that strategy is leading to your ultimate HD Destination. Tracing that line in reverse is also how pilots regain situational awareness from a tumbleweed situation, when we've all but lost our handle on what we are doing. Losing situational awareness is like being lost on a hike. To regain your bearings, find something big (a mountain top), before focussing on the smaller things (a creek and your trail). We call it 'Big to Small'. The HD Destination is your mountain. It answers your purpose, explains your mission, and guides what you should be doing now.

Remember the mission to bomb all the ball bearing factories in Schweinfurt, Germany in World War II. It was brilliantly executed to bomb the factories, but that should not have been the intended effect. If the idea was to deny ball bearings to the German military, bombing the factories did nothing—there were already stockpiles of bearings all over Germany. Unfortunately, those planning the mission didn't have line-of-sight alignment through to the effect they were aiming for. Somewhere along the line, it was blocked.

To some extent we are all effects-based thinkers. If you were ever watching a movie late at night and muttered to yourself 'C'mon—it's not that great a movie—gotta get going in the morning—big day', then you're thinking of effects. Teenagers seem to lose that ability for a while, but as we mature, we think more and more of effects. We get support from our parents, our peers, mentors, and schools to learn how to do that, and can do it when we make the effort.

Yet few individuals or organizations think of effects systematically. We just push ahead with what needs to be done immediately. There are two reasons for this. More often than we'd like to admit, it's because we don't have an ultimate end in mind. We're not really aiming for anything. We're just getting through the school week, or the term, or to the end of the year, or to long-service leave. We're on a treadmill and it's taking us . . . somewhere.

Just as likely, we have this week's objective in sight and an ultimate end in mind, but haven't thought through how to get from one to the other. We need to be able to visualise that path, to create and follow a long-term plan. A leader needs to have line of sight between what they're doing now and what they want in the future. Are your actions taking you closer or further away? Are you building the skills and relationships to get there? Are you building the personal and team culture to get there?

This means that all of our actions have their direct effects (immediate things like appointing a person to a position) and indirect effects (people being disappointed to miss out on that position, team results improving or deteriorating, resources being spent on training the new person, other actions). They have intended effects (a team has a new leader, team results improving) and unintended effects (team morale falling, results improving for unforeseen reasons).

What we are looking to do is to get a greater handle on those effects. In the planning stage of Flex, you'll get the opportunity to think through the effects in advance. But when you're on a mission, you have to do it on the run. You want it to be second nature, well-rehearsed.

SYSTEMS THINKING

Systems thinking can't be underestimated, but can be overcomplicated. Academics will rave about the intricacies of networks and systems, and the great many relationships and complexities they generate. That may well be true. But what we're looking for is a way to think of systems simply, to help us make the right decisions in both planning and executing our missions.

To start thinking of systems, think of how different people might respond to an action you take. For example, say your mission is to fill an important position in your company. In that case, the system will include your company, the people in it, and the professionals who could fill that position. If you advertize the position, how will your own people respond? If a lot of them come knocking on your door, how will you respond? If the professionals know you've got six qualified people within your company, how will they respond?

You can see that each action we take, each direct and indirect effect, takes place within a system. Everything we see and do is part of not just one system, but a hierarchy of systems. Our physical body is an atom in a cell in a bloodstream in a leg in a body in a person in a family in a community. Our economic person is a buyer from or employee in a company in a market in a state in a national in a global economy.

For most people, the best way to understand the system they're in—or the one they want to create—is to draw it. This is what Walt Disney did in 1957. By then he had been making animated movies for 30 years, and been *the* player in animation for twenty years, since *Snow White and the Seven Dwarfs* was released in 1937. But he had an idea for a theme park, for Disneyland, and needed a map to show his team how it all fit together, and therefore what they had to do to create the new Disney system. Figure 14 is that map.

Granted, you may not be able to draw like Walt, but you can draw system maps for your company and its markets. We'll have a look at another in the next chapter. They key thing is to draw connections until you and your team understands the system

Figure 14: Map of Disneyland theme park

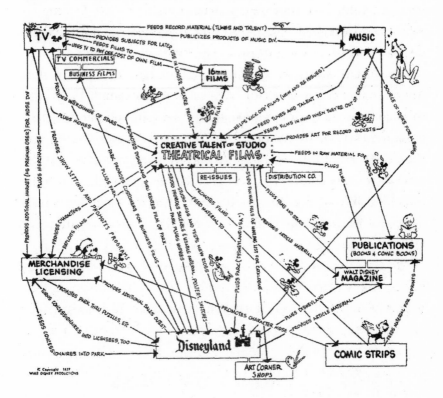

Source: © 1957 Disney.

they're in, and is aware of how one change in the system may have unintended consequences for another part of the system.

This is the type of thinking that, for all their other enormous talents, seemed to be missing at Blockbuster when Netflix CEO Reed Hastings came knocking in the year 2000.[1] At the time, Netflix was a dot.com startup, and Blockbuster was the dominant gorilla in the video entertainment industry, worth about U.S.$2.8 billion. Hastings thought that the combination of Netflix and Blockbuster would be unbeatable in the transition from store to online video. Blockbuster thought that the online minnow wouldn't challenge the stores and, if it did, that Blockbuster itself could set up its own online service. Netflix wouldn't have the firepower to respond to that, they thought.

But Blockbuster wasn't thinking enough of the main player in the system—the customer. The Netflix model of monthly subscriptions would get rid of what customers hated most: fees for the late return of videos. Customers responded by signing up. Blockbuster had to respond, and eventually in 2006 its CEO dropped the late fees and started an online service. Yet the late fees delivered Blockbuster most and arguably *all* of its profits, and setting up the online service was expensive: four times as much as buying out Netflix in 2000. So the CEO then hit a response from the internal players of Blockbuster's system, who were scared that they were spending more money just as their profitability was evaporating. They pushed him out, and reversed his decisions. But Netflix had already irreversibly changed their system, and the old ways no longer worked. Blockbuster was bankrupt shortly afterwards.

BUILDING SITUATIONAL AWARENESS

Situational awareness sounds like wisdom: a perception that's cheap in hindsight but extremely rare and valuable in foresight. Are some people born lucky with situational awareness? Perhaps. More likely they have disciplined themselves to think about things in a structured way. Experience is certainly a factor—the greybeards who 'have been around a long time'. But without curiosity and a way to meld past experience with new data, you're likely to be sunk in the mire.

We strongly believe that Flex itself provides the disciplined process and expansive thinking that helps build situational awareness. The Flex engine of plan–brief–execute–debrief matches the ways in which adults learn best. In planning, we *consider* new things collaboratively and expansively, taking in outside advice, and *processing* those ideas into a specific, actionable course of action. In the brief, we *hear* the leader's synthesis of the plan, stressing elements of situational awareness that will make a difference to the mission. In executing the mission, we *experience* the very things that beforehand only existed in concept, in our minds. We add our own perspectives regarding the situation to our learning, direct experience rather than indirect. And in the debrief, we *review* those perspectives, learning from cause and effect, finding out that two people can perceive the very same event quite differently, and how to reconcile those perceptions.

For some missions, all the situational awareness you need should be in the room, or readily accessible within your organization. For others, tap into external experts to help build that awareness. There will be things you don't know about—both known unknowns and unknown unknowns—that will have a material impact on the outcome of your missions that make it up. If the mission of your team of six inhouse IT specialists is to upgrade your data center with new hardware and expanded storage capacity, you will have the expertise you need. If your strategy is to move that data center to a new location, at the same time transitioning to a mix of proprietary hardware and vendor-owned infrastructure accessing both proprietary and public cloud, then you will need to draw on external experts.

Having situational awareness is one thing; using it is quite another. We also think of situational awareness as 'perception, comprehension, and projection'—see, think and act. Most people can see or perceive things happening, fewer will understand or comprehend what that means, and fewer still will project into the future to make decisions on what to do about it. When the U.S. Coast Guard cutter *Cuyahoga* approached the Argentinean vessel M/V *Santa Cruz II* on a clear, calm night on the Chesapeake Bay in 1978, both crews saw each other by eye and by radar. Everyone had that perception. When the *Cuyahoga's* captain turned his ship in front of the *Santa Cruz*, all of his crew saw it, and many would have understood what the change of course meant. But all assumed he had his reasons and neither warned nor questioned him. 'So they just stood there and let it happen'—'it' being the *Cuyahogo* rammed and eleven lives lost.[2] If there was perception on the *Cuyahoga's* bridge, there was little comprehension and certainly not enough projection.

Situational awareness is the eyes and ears of your mission. It takes in what's around you now, as well as what's in front of you—all the way to your mission objective.

FLEX IN ORGANIZATIONS

As we keep stressing, Flex works at the individual, the team, and the organizational levels. To this point, this book has mainly focussed on what Flex delivers for the team and the individual, leaders and their highly valued followers. Our next challenge is to consider Flex from the organization's perspective. That is not a trivial shift in perspective, but it should be a smooth one. Flex is *designed* to be a scalable approach to thought and action, which is why its principles are used so extensively in the military and now in business. It is designed to be used independently or in unison by multiple teams at any level of an organization. When used in unison, its teams and objectives aligned with their ultimate objective, their execution rhythms in sync, Flex can generate enormous energy within your organization.

The Maple Flag

The first time Murph saw the full force of a disciplined process at international scale, was in the NATO-wide exercises held at Cold Lake Air Force Base, Canada—The Maple Flag.

'Every fighter pilot can talk about his or her first Flag exercise, and this was mine. I took my F-15 Eagle up as part of two Blue four-ships, supporting a large strike force aiming to take out Red targets. It was much different from flying at home, with the standard procedures and the standard rigor, at the standard airfield with the standard calls going into our standard base, going in against the standard F-15s or the standard F/A-18 Hornets that the Marines flew. For the first time I was going to have to deploy, plan a mission, and in very short order execute it, because every night we'd get our fragmentary order, part of a much broader strategy, and our commanders would have to find a place in it for all our units. Maple Flags teach air crews not only how to react, but how to plan in the overall scheme of a battle plan. It was a new environment for us, with many air forces speaking different languages, using different types of radios and weapons, different radar systems, intercepts and ground control procedures. The one comforting factor for me was the process. Everybody was using a basic form of what I would come to describe as Flex. The overall exercise would be broken down into campaigns, and then into separate missions. Every day, there was a mass debriefing, and then team debriefings on our individual missions. It was overwhelming to see each day's planning cascade down to the mission level, and the debriefs cascade back up to help reset the next day's events. It was an immense amount of pressure, but the calming event was that we were all prepared. We had all memorized the standard operating procedures for the Maple Flag, so that going to and from this strange airfield, with unfamiliar squadron all coming back low on fuel after our missions, seemed to go like clockwork. Because we were debriefing every single day, our performance as a squadron and as a force kept getting stronger and stronger as the days went on. And although it was more chaotic and high pressure than anything I'd ever experienced, the calming thread was the process and the standards, which reset the baseline of basic execution.'

In this chapter, we will put Flex in the context of a larger organization with a focus on one critical question: if Flex is the ideal approach to get things done, can a company use it to execute its corporate strategy? We believe it can, because we've seen it happen time after time. There are three things to consider:

1. **The organizational objective.** A larger organization will have as its corporate mission or strategy something more complex than the clear, single objective of a team mission. Flex can work on an organizational objective with many facets. But each facet must still be clear, measurable and achievable. That's what we call a High-definition Destination (HD), and Flex can get you there.

2. **Long-term missions.** Achieving a corporate strategy or HD Destination doesn't happen overnight. Yet the same principles that underpin Flex still apply.

3. **Missions to change your system.** More often than not, the whole point of an organizational strategy is to change something about the system in which it operates. That takes a little extra bit of thinking, but that's only a small extension of Flex planning.

Don't get us wrong. We know how complex organizational strategy and change can be: we've seen them in action countless times. We know the detailed U.S. and Australian approaches to nationwide military planning and execution. We don't pretend that Flex is a substitute for either of them, if they're really needed. Our point is that they're not often needed. In most organizations, most of the time, Flex will be more than enough.

SETTING A HIGH-DEFINITION (HD) DESTINATION

While Flex can be directed at any organizational future, it helps that everyone in the organization has a really clear, high-definition picture of that destination.

Some companies have great visions. Amazon's vision is 'to be earth's most customer-centric company; to build a place where people can come to find and discover anything they might want to buy online.'[1] We now know what that vision looks like—like Amazon.com. But before it was built? Could the leaders at Amazon tell you exactly what they were building?

The Flex HD Destination defines fundamental goals that together make certain what you're offering to what market, how you'll be perceived, who works for you and how they'll do it well, how you're structured, and what your financial performance will be. It's not so detailed that it limits people's creativity; nor is it so fuzzy that it allows creativity to prejudice performance. Just right, so that a team leader on a mission can make a judgment call that their mission may no longer be heading for the HD Destination.

Dan McAtee found himself in need of an HD Destination when he became president of a major international steel company, with operations in 35 countries including the U.S., Colombia, England, Pakistan, and Vietnam. His challenge was to align these diverse groups of facilities and employees with clear goals. That was never going to be easy, so Dan chose to beat complexity with simplicity. He got everyone he needed into the one room—people representing the different countries, functions, levels, and specialities inside and outside the firm—to create a shared HD Destination.

It took them two days, and at the end they had an HD Destination that they owned, collectively and individually. McAtee called it a 75 percent plan, and that was enough. 'Working with other methodologies, I've spent too much time trying to get perfect data. You just can't do it or do it expediently. And I'm a Six Sigma black belt! So we all came up with a simple plan together. It got us moving together in a common direction, accountable to one another. And the process builds in feedback and adjustment, so we'll figure out the remaining 25 percent as we go. The important thing is that we're moving forward together. We started allocating limited resources in an effective way and avoiding fights! Our alignment vastly improved decision-making because we could test options against our agreed HD Destination.'

The real test came, though, then the financial markets melted down in 2008. 'When the financial crisis came, this process kept the company above water,' said McAtee. 'Our demand dropped by 20 percent, but we still grew at 5 percent, even in that environment. Our people could execute against our plan and make needed adjustments locally, since they were empowered and understood the HD Destination.'[2]

What we're looking for in an HD Destination is a sense of purpose that compels us rationally and practically, as well as emotionally and inspirationally. It's a vision of the future that all who choose to work with us can get behind. Such a vision helps to 'direct, align and inspire actions on the part of large numbers of people,' says John Kotter,[3] and that's exactly what we want.

Achieving such an HD Destination is a fine balance. General, inspirational visions can set the purpose of a company or community, but they're not enough. Here are two great visions that, different as they are, would both inspire us, and be a standard against which we can test everything we do:

'I have a dream that my four little children will one day live in a nation where they will not be judged by the color of their skin, but by the content of their character.'[4]

'At the Coca-Cola Company we strive to refresh the world, inspire moments of optimism and happiness, create value and make a difference.'[5]

These visions give us identity and purpose, and are invaluable both for the people pursuing them and for the communities they serve. They go beyond 'being the best at what we do', and state that 'what we do matters'. A telco might say 'we have the best mobile network in the land', or it might say 'we connect people'.

Yet pure as these visions are in *purpose*, would they be enough to guide decision-making on all matters and at all levels of your company or community? We need a little more context and detail, but not too much. We need the vision to be clear, so that it is not confusing or difficult to implement. And we want it to be expressed in simple terms so that anyone in the organization can describe it.

Set a clear HD Destination, and people will rally round to make it real. Leave it vague and people may draw their own conclusions. Every second episode of your favorite TV sit-com is built around people going off and doing very different things after hearing the same vague direction. As fighter pilots, it wasn't so funny. If we knew exactly what our leaders wanted on the battlefield, then they could rest easy at night knowing it would get done. If we didn't have that clearly in mind, then they may wake up to the news that the wrong target had been hit.

Five elements of the HD Destination for an organization

It is not easy to paint a vision of something as complex as an organization, with all the uncertainty of the future, and all the possibilities available. What would you include, and what would you leave out?

We've spent twenty years boiling down what you could possibly put into your HD Destination into five key areas or elements. Our chosen elements started life 60 years ago, when Peter Drucker set out eight key areas of management in his monumental 1954 work, *The Practice of Management*. They were refined by Drucker himself in subsequent editions, then by others, and most recently by John A. Warden and Leland A. Russell.[6] And we've kept tightening them up.

Here are our five elements, and their component dimensions, that guide us through what may be important to an organization. They may not be the only way of looking at things, and your own organization may have more or less elements, or express them differently. But we offer them to you as a strong place to start:

1. **Competitive position.** The *markets* we're in (businesses and geographies) notionally multiplied by our *profile* in them (our business model, competitive advantage, brand).
2. **Productivity.** The *skills* our people have (their lived experience, and inherent and learned abilities) notionally multiplied by their *will* in using it (the culture, engagement, and benefits we can offer).
3. **Entrepreneurship.** Our capacity for *innovation* (culture, autonomy, R&D) notionally multiplied by our appetite for *risk* (controls, standards, processes, ratios).

4. **Capital productivity.** The financial capital we invest (debt, equity, reinvested revenue) multiplied by the return on that investment (ROIC, margin).

5. **Asset ownership.** Our legal structures (legal entity, employee shares, mergers and acquisitions growth) for the assets we own (businesses, property, infrastructure, intellectual property).

Elements such as these define an organization and can guide focussed planning and action. A traditional, broader vision complements the Flex HD Destination well: you do not have to replace what is treasured. But you will find it extremely hard to execute your strategy unless you have an HD Destination in place. You can use the Flex process to develop an HD Destination, or you can test the vision you have and fill in the gaps. Either way there's work, very achievable work, to be done.

Clear, measurable, achievable elements

Just as a mission objective needs to be clear, measurable, and achievable, so too do the elements of the HD Destination. That's the surest way to prepare for the mission objectives to be aligned with the HD Destination, which is the whole point of the mission.

As with mission objectives, the components of each HD Destination element should be absolute, not relative to a market or an economy. Make them about your sales, not your rank in the market. Markets are not zero sum games: company performance is in part dependent on industry performance, and both you and your competition may do extremely well in a year that's good for your industry. Put a stake in the ground with specific numbers, rather than calling for 'more than last year', and adjust those numbers with each year's strategy cycle as you need to.

You can see how similar the dimensions of an HD Destination are to mission objectives. They are the very peak of the mission objectives, the targets and destinations to which all the other objectives are aimed. But just like mission objectives, there is nothing in them about *how* those dimensions will be pursued or met. That's for the teams at the highest level of the organization to decide, with their decisions cascading down through the teams at every level.

Setting your HD Destination

As we've seen, the HD Destination is made up of five elements that each contain a small selection of measurable objectives. Setting a company's HD Destination is remarkably similar to mission planning—which is not surprising given that this is Flex.

The main steps towards creating and testing an HD Destination are as follows:

1. **Get the right team in place.** Here we ask the same questions as in mission planning. Who will be involved in achieving the HD Destination? Do they have the situational awareness they need to assess the trends and threats that will affect the company over the next three years or more? If specialists are needed to fill in that situational awareness, who can we bring in? This is open planning at the most important level, so make sure you have who you need in the room.
2. **Tap into your situational awareness.** Consider not just how the company has recently fared, but the trends and threats on the horizon. Allow for discussion: the team has to have a common view of your position and possibilities.
3. **Confirm your organizational identity: your purpose or mission.** Why does your company exist? Is it to create wealth, offer fulfillment for its owners and employees, give customers a unique experience, be part of a fabulous industry, do something valuable for the community or the world? The Coca-Cola Company may want to 'refresh the world and inspire moments

of optimism and happiness', but it needs an HD Destination for what it will be as a company to be able to do that. The two statements go together, and you won't have an actionable HD Destination unless you have a clear purpose or mission to connect with.

4. **Ensure the HD Destination dimensions are clear, measurable, achievable, and aligned.** For each of the five pairs of HD Destination dimensions listed above, decide what is most important to have in place, and test that it is clear, measurable, and achievable. And that, when taken together, they are aligned: that is, they are mutually consistent, and can support each other.

5. **Review your HD Destination and organizational identity as one vision.** Stand back and consider your confirmed identity and new three-year HD Destination together. Do they fit as one? Will they both guide and inspire? Is that something your team can *do*? Who will be happy if you achieve it? Who may not be, and does that matter?

That's quite a session you've just completed. We've been part of hundreds like it, and each time the energy that comes from that room overwhelms the energy that went in. If you get this right, you're well on the way to your HD Destination.

MISSIONS TO REACH THE HD DESTINATION

It's likely that the HD Destination you've set for your company, or the strategy you already have, is not a simple set of tasks. It will take time, effort, and many teams to achieve. Yet we've been talking all along about specific missions, missions with a tight objective that a single team can achieve in a day, a week, or a month. It's clear that reaching an HD Destination is going to take many such missions, and that they may be spread over the timeframe of the HD Destination or strategy—up to three years. They will likely be the responsibility of the company's most senior executives. Those higher-level missions will rely on other missions to be completed by executives on the next level of management, and so on through the organization.

So missions need to be launched up and down the company. Don't be hung up on what you call those missions. For the team planning and carrying them out, they are just missions, and they will all Flex them in exactly the same way. Distinguishing between, say, strategic or tactical missions is misleading. A strategic mission for one level of management is a tactical mission for the next level up. That's just the way organizations are structured, and why they are so powerful—if all those missions are aligned.

The missions have one thing in common. Every mission has to align with the HD Destination. Every mission that takes place in an organization must have in its line of sight the ultimate HD Destination of the organization. There is an immediate, measurable, and achievable objective for that mission. But in the planning and conduct of that mission there will be choices to make. To help make them, the team has to have an eye on what the missions and strategies higher up in the organization are aiming to do, all the way up to the HD Destination. That's the guiding light, the light on the hill, without which situational awareness is impossible.

Consider Figure 15, 'Mission alignment'. On the left is the current state of too many organizations. Teams are doing things, but many are doing their own things.

The situation means that the planning and conduct of the mission must ask: what is the effect of a particular action? Will that effect help the organization's objectives, directly and indirectly, one, two, or three levels above? If it does, go for it. If it doesn't, tread very carefully. This takes a lot of situational awareness.

Figure 15: Mission alignment

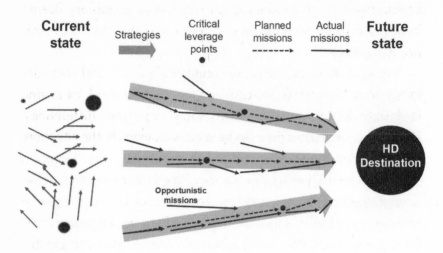

Source: Afterburner Inc.

Consider a mission to build a factory to a set of clear specifications. That's a mission, with a measurable objective. But it is not an end in itself—you are not building a factory for its own sake. You are building the factory because the company wants to increase its production, or to shift its production, or to make a different product. That's the intended effect you're looking for, and it's the objective of the team that ordered the factory built. But that's not an end in itself either. Why increase production? Because it will help fill orders to meet the goal of increased revenue, and that's the mission and objective of the team that's ordered the increased production. Why increase revenue? Because the revenue objective is part of the HD Destination, one of the company's performance goals, and that's why the CEO asked for it. Why? So that investors will continue to invest in the company, providing jobs for its people, serving the needs of its customers.

Is that the end of the story? No. The people designing the factory need situational awareness of the other missions that are pushing towards the HD Destination. They may relate to the culture (open sight or silo), business model (made-to-order or commodity), or product quality. Choices in factory design have to take into account these objectives, just as much as their immediate objective.

Some of these missions are completed quickly, and some are longer-term. You won't be surprised to read that the Flex engine is designed to power both, with some important differences. Essentially, the longer time frame means changes in the situation, the team and other resources, and the objectives over that time.

Over a longer period, the surrounding environment changes. Competitors or investors may come and go. Crises may arise elsewhere in the business to take away people and resources. Changes in regulations may demand more or less compliance cost. People may leave for other pastures. All of this means that a mission objective and plan will change. The original measure may become too easy due to breakthroughs elsewhere or in its own missions, or too hard. A better way of reaching objectives may be discovered, as new resources become available. The X-Gaps review progress of the course of action, but are more likely to update the objective and plan.

STRATEGIC MISSIONS TO CREATE YOUR SYSTEM

If a team reaches its objective through its mission plan, a company reaches its HD Destination through its strategy. Strategic planning is mission planning writ large. If it's successful, every team in the business will be pulling in the same direction. So, how does a strategy reach the HD Destination?

The way we look at it, whatever business you're in, wherever you are, you're operating within a system. As we saw in the previous chapter, you need to understand your system to operate effectively in it. That's part of your situational awareness. You need to know your system even better if you want to change it. Systems are constantly adjusting: every move you or someone else makes tweaks the system. But all the bonds and relationships in a system are elastic. Make a small move, and the elastic bonds give a little, then ease back to where they were. If you want to change the system, you have to apply enough force, at the right place, for those bonds to break. That's what you may need to do to reach your HD Destination: apply pressure at the right places to change the system you're in now, into what you want it to be. These are the system's critical leverage points, and that's what your strategy should be targeting.

This is how 'Gusto' built the strategy for an innovative startup company in the ultracompetitive car repair industry.[7] Dent Recon sent mobile technicians with small-area repair techniques (SMART) to client sites to quickly restore a vehicle's exterior panels. It was an invaluable service for car rental clients in particular, so they could return a car with a minor dent quickly to the fleet. Having bedded down that technology, Dent Recon wanted to ramp up their business with high-tech, SMART repair service centers, set up to turn cars around much more quickly than traditional repairers, for both consumers and car rental firms. To understand how the new Dent Recon system would work, Gusto drew a systems map (also called an 'influence map'), and used it to help the team build, understand, and commit to the new strategy: see Figure 16.

Using their influence map, the Dent Recon team identified the three critical leverage points that would guide their strategy, the three points with the most connections: the SMART repair service centers, the skills and reliability of the technicians who worked there, and the tools and equipment they would use. The company launched missions to get these three things to the standards called for in their HD Destination. They realized that each of these strategic missions had the intended effect of driving

Figure 16: Dent Recon influence map

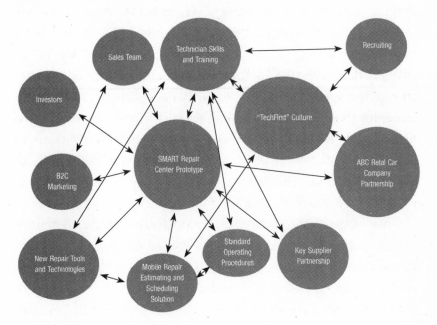

Source: Afterburner Inc.

quality in their technician's work. In fact, that became the focus of Dent Recon's strategy and culture: 'Technicians first.' They could prioritize their missions by how much they could support technicians in delivering quality to their customers, without which they wouldn't stay long in business.

As CEO of the startup, Gusto learned that he could not repeat the company's HD Destination and strategy often enough. His team heard them at every Flex session—the planning sessions, the briefs, and the debriefs. Yet it wasn't always Gusto doing the talking. At every session he asked a different person in the team to spell it out, so that they knew what their mission was aiming for, they could plan for it, take ownership of it, and make the right decisions on the run. That simple yet essential practice kept his efforts pointing at the critical leverage points, and through them to the HD Destination.

Finding critical leverage points

Put simply, critical leverage points are those points in the system that are connected most to other points. They are the points on the influence map that have the most lines to them. If the system won't work without them, they're the points to take out (to destroy the current system) or set in place (to build your new system).

Examples abound. We've talked about the Schweinfurt ball bearing factories in World War II (and why the strategy to take them out failed, see Chapter 7, 'The six-step mission planning process'). Every German tank, plane, train, and car had a line drawn to those factories. More recently, Colonel John Warden attacked critical leverage points to devastating effect in Operation Desert Storm, the aerial bombing centerpiece of the 1991 Gulf War. The campaign planners had identified over 300,000 potential military, power, communication, and transportation targets—way too many to focus the aerial campaign on. What were the critical leverage points? The power plants, certainly. But they were heavily defended, and would take weeks of saturation bombing to overcome. What else? The power grid itself could be attacked, but electricity could always find a new path through the grid, and power wires could be quickly restored. One planner had a better idea. Throughout the grid were a limited number of 'step-up transformers', the points where power from the generating plants is aggregated and then redistributed through the grid. Knock out the transformers, and you've knocked out the grid, and it won't be easy to reboot it. They were the critical leverage points, and they weren't heavily defended. That's exactly where Colonel Warden struck. The lights were put out in Iraq in a single night.

In business, the critical leverage points can be within your own company or they can be external. As highways were rolled out over post-war America, Walmart saw the opportunity to place huge department stores along these highways on the outskirts of town, rather than buy up little spaces in the town centers.

The external points were those ideal highway sites, and also the regulations that in the 1960s restricted retail premises from using those sites. Change those regulations and you've changed the system, so Walmart lobbied hard to make those changes. Of course, Walmart would have had to plan for the most likely responses as part of their course of action, and for others as contingencies. If they had competitors, they had to think how those competitors would respond. 'Competitive moves by one firm . . . may incite retaliation or efforts to counter the move; that is, firms are mutually dependent.'[8] As we've seen, Flex planning foresees these risks and contingencies, and plans for them.

Finding the critical leverage point was the issue that faced Boo's company Mode in Papua New Guinea, not the easiest place in the world to do business. Following his in Afghanistan, Boo was invited to advise on airport security in Port Moresby. Like many others, he saw an opportunity there in property: a construction boom in the city to house workers and contracting firms for the ExxonMobil natural gas project that was renewing the country's economy. Yet because of that boom, everything in Port Moresby was expensive. Fuel, materials, labor, expertize—anything you needed had to be imported, profit margins along the chain were exorbitant, and the economics of construction were terrible. In the influence map of Boo's system, everything was linked to construction cost, and that leverage point was ugly.

His solution? Build as much as possible overseas, and ship 80 percent-complete rooms and units to Port Moresby as modules. This was a whole new way of modular construction. It needed a clear course of action for the logistics and building certification, but the economics worked. Unfortunately for the project, Exxon had reduced their footprint and the project was shelved, downsized and sold to a local investor. During this R and D process, Boo became convinced that modular construction was the future, not only in Papua New Guinea, but anywhere in the world. He established Mode Developments with Sydney-based property developers, the Molyneux Group, and invested in what was at the time a small 14-story hotel project in Perth CBD. The project was completely redesigned and is now the tallest modular hotel in the world. It would not have existed without identifying the critical leverage points of a construction system, and using the Flex process to adapt the plan to real world changes, and execute the course of action.

CAN YOU OWN AND EXECUTE YOUR STRATEGY?

Imagining your future HD Destination, mapping out systems, identifying the critical leverage points, working out missions—this is the stuff of strategy. We've seen that a strategic mission is one that targets a critical leverage point to shape the system in the way you want it shaped. A corporate strategy, as most people understand it, is made up of these strategic missions (and the ongoing pay-the-bills operational missions). As we've seen, you can use Flex to develop that strategy for your company or organization. Just as likely, you have a strategy team—internal or external—who are proposing a strategy to you. No matter how good that strategy may be, you need to answer the following questions:

- Do our people know and own this strategy?
- How can we execute this strategy?

These are the questions that VMware, a U.S. software firm, faced in 2015. It had developed a robust corporate strategy with the help of a specialist strategy consulting firm. Nobody questioned the direction and potential value of that strategy, and the executive were keen to make it happen. The only problem was that, like many such strategies, it was *very* comprehensive and not a little complicated. Under four pillars of intended effects, there were over 200 initiatives, both strategic and operational. A first cut at prioritization by the strategy team got that list down to 33: manageable but still too many for the firm to focus on.

VMware then applied Flex to the strategy itself. Its executive was the team responsible for delivering the strategy, so they set themselves that mission, and set about creating a mission plan using Flex, just as Chapter 7 lays out. The first step was to ensure they defined a clear, measurable, achievable objective: the HD Destination of this strategy. They could then work through the threats that strategy faced, the resources and lessons learned they could draw on, their course of action for getting it done (who would be responsible to do what by when), their execution rhythm for X-Gaps on the whole strategy, a Red Team to test all that, and the contingencies they could allow for.

Scott Bajtos was the Chief Customer Officer at VMware leading the process. 'Our organizations typically go through changes and have silos that are built up over time. The problem I was trying to solve was to see through the chaos and rise above it all, to create a very simple HD Destination at the highest level, with a set of principles to set us up for success. I go back to one of our tenets: focus on what we can control. The whole mission was a driving force for clarity. To me, any methodology that can drive clarity in the organization with accountability built into it—it's just a big win.'[9]

Their 33 initiatives, major pieces of work, were all targeted at critical leverage points to create the system that was their HD Destination. Who was to say that one initiative was more important than another? The only people who could determine that were the people who were responsible for implementing them: themselves. They had to understand what the initiatives were, and make their own decisions on what to do with them. They discussed them enough to understand each one, and prioritized them in the same way the team prioritized anything: comparing their cost and effort to implement against their potential value to the company. By discussing each initiative enough to be able to prioritize them within a single course of action, they also better understood the strategy as a whole.

VMware was then also set to execute those initiatives, using the same Flex methodology that give clarity to their strategy. Scott Bajtos found that the Flex engine offered discipline traction on missions as diverse as innovation and service. 'We created a fast-lane support app for our premier service customers. When they were in a priority-one situation, a production-down environment, they didn't have anything other than the phone or email to reach us. So we created an app that automatically opens the request and dials to someone who answers within 30 seconds. The next version of the app was our cloud command center, building technology into our products for us to predict an outage before a customer's even experience it. By applying the Flex model—planning, briefing, red-teaming, everything—we were able to produce a beta that looks very promising for us, by acquiring a company with technology that we can bolt onto VMware. That was something we could never have done before. We would have eventually come to the conclusion, but it would have been a much longer runway. The pace with which we were able to drive an outcome with this level of commitment was based solely on the Flex model.'

Is your strategy ready to be executed with similar out-of-the-box thinking and commitment? Let's go back to the beginning. Flex works because it puts in place a series of critical balances to engage people, cut through complexity, and get things done. It balances speed and awareness, so that the right decisions are made while getting things done. It balances simple and dynamic, so that there are clear plans to act under uncertainty, and can change course when you must. And it balances the direct and empowering, so that people have both the autonomy and the accountability to be fully engaged in their mission.

The same things that achieve this balance through a mission, can do so for a strategy. That means the same things need to be in place. You cannot expect your team to execute a complex corporate strategy in uncertain times unless you can answer 'yes' to the following questions. It's not a problem if you can't—you just have a little work to do before your strategy is ready to execute. But you have to get to that point.

All of the following questions center on your executive team, the people who will be executing the strategy. Just like a team setting out on a daily mission, this is the only team that matters:

1. Has your executive team taken the strategy as your leader's intent, and created an HD Destination, each part of which is clear, measurable, and achievable, as the ultimate objective of the strategy?

2. Has your executive team identified the threats to achieving that HD Destination? To do so, has it mapped the system in which the HD Destination will sit, and identified the likely responses from those in the system?

3. Has your executive team identified the resources and lessons it has learned to overcome those threats and achieve the HD Destination?

4. Has your executive team identified and prioritized the strategic initiatives into a course of action, nominating the individuals and the timeframe to do them?

5. Has an independent, external Red Team stress-tested that course of action?

6. Has your executive team reviewed the course of action in light of the Red Team review, and built in contingencies?

7. Does the course of action set an execution rhythm with regular X-Gap reviews?

8. Are there universally agreed standards in place—processes, culture, communications—by which the initiatives and X-Gap reviews will be conducted?

If you can answer 'yes' to all these questions, then you as CEO are ready to stamp your personal mark on the strategy, and *brief* the course of action to your executive team. Then there are two more questions to follow up on within a month of the brief:

1. Does each individual who is accountable for an initiative have a clear dashboard to track its performance?
2. Does each individual who is accountable for an initiative have a peer wingman to offer mutual support?

You won't be surprised to see that these are not random questions. They align with the Flex engine for flawless execution, the engine at the core of Flex and of this book. This is the engine that works, and will power you through your strategy. Just don't jump to execution before you have planned and briefed, just like any other Flex mission.

14

THE FLEX WINGS

For Flex, our wings are the standards we set for our processes and culture, the training we hone to meet them, and the systems we use to access them. We don't get far without our wings, so we invest to make them strong.

Strong wings are essential. Apart from keeping you in the air, which is nice, they keep you steady when there's turbulence. They also set boundaries for what you try out in the cockpit: you can't do anything that the wings can't handle. The whole machine may fall apart.

The Flex way of thinking allows you to rely on your wings, the simple certainty of your standards, so you can take on complex uncertainties. Keep your mind free for the hard stuff. Albert Einstein was famous for saying, 'Never memorize something that you can look up,' when he couldn't tell a colleague his own phone number. That was sound advice when you were living in the 1920s, tackling the hardest problems known to mankind, working by yourself, surrounded by the few reference books you need, with all the time in the world. Whether or not we're in a jet fighter, our reality today is a little different. We work in teams, under time pressure, with infinite data available. If we stopped to look everything up, we would slow down the team, and most likely embarrass ourselves.

THE LAYERS OF STANDARDS AND LEARNING

To understand how a company can best build wings, and you can best use them, we need to make a few distinctions:

- There are organizational standards that have to be memorized, and training is essential to help them sink in. Training equals habits and new habits equal new behaviors.
- There are organizational standards and knowledge that you can look up, as long as there's some way to look them up in a hurry. This includes all the lessons learned and situational awareness that your company can draw on.
- There are personal standards—habits and techniques—that we rely on individually, but that can't interfere with the organizational standards.
- There is personal initiative and creativity, all that goes on in the cockpit, which is what everything else is there to support.

That's how Flex performance is built. We layer one set of abilities on top of the other, and keep learning.

Let's take the example of a production team at a snack-food company, and the mass production of perhaps 50 different treats. Their base is what they do with their time and machines every day—their organizational standards: non-negotiable, structurally sound, memorized, used every day, always at the ready. These keep the snacks coming off the production line when and as they're required, in the quality set for them.

Next is situational standards and awareness. Something happens that doesn't occur every day: a new product being trialled, a stoppage on a line, an ingredient failing a quality test, a person missing in a critical role. In these regular and defined situations, the team needs to draw on particular standards and knowledge that they don't memorize, but can tap into quickly. These are standards and lessons learned by the whole company. The team doesn't have to reinvent the wheel, but the wheel has to be in the garage ready to roll.

Our personal habits and techniques can have the same positive influence as standards. They can steady us for action, get us through situations quickly, calm our nerves, improve our personal performance, and ready us for creativity. When a mission plan calls us to do something, it tells us *what* to do, not *how* to do it. We're told to get a car to a certain place at a certain time, not how to drive that car. Even while following checklists to start up or cool down a production plant, each of us will have individual habits that we rely on to look at and check our equipment—*as long as they are consistent with the checklist itself.* Organizational standards first, personal habits second.

These are the wings that as a company, and individually, you work on. They're the ones that you want to be able to rely on without thinking. When you have to deal with a situation that's new, in planning or in action, you need your wings to be strong, so that you can act with all the awareness, initiative, and creativity you can muster—for that's what you need to win in an uncertain world.

STANDARDS

Standards ensure that each person on the team knows the process, and relies on the others to also know the process. They cut about two-thirds of the time needed for any discussion, and two-thirds of the risks from any mission.

Working to standards gives a team enormous confidence in facing new situations. When those standards are known and trained across an organization, they are powerful. They don't have to be complicated: their power comes from being able to rely on them, absolutely, any time. As fighter pilots, our common standards allow us to work with pilots from other squadrons, bases, and air forces, if need be at a moment's notice. We can trust the other pilots with our lives, because they know the standards.

We want to share two examples to demonstrate how valuable standards are to us: one that happens every day, one from a day we hope never happens again.

At Afterburner, we facilitate planning and debrief sessions all over the U.S. on a daily basis, sometimes with new clients, sometimes with people we've worked with for years. We stick to the same standard every time, no matter how many times we've done it: work with a wingman, get there at a certain time the day before, contact the team on arrival, inspect the client rooms and technology, brief at the same time that night, arrive at the client site the same time in the morning, the same dress standards, the same communication signals and codes, the same debrief afterwards. That's our starting point. Throughout our planning and preparation time, we'll make adjustments to best suit our client and situation. But that's what we start with, and we cannot stress enough the confidence and the comfort that gives. Like all facilitators, we're nervous. We want to do a good job and we know we're fallible. Our standards keep us from guessing and wasting time on the small stuff, so we can concentrate on the substance of what we're doing. That's what we're getting paid for.

On one of these days, 10 September 2001, one of our pilots gave a seminar in upstate New York, staying the night after in nearby Burlington, Vermont. The morning after, the pilot, 'Bourke', boarded his plane for the next seminar in Houston. Out of nowhere, air traffic control put everybody on hold, so our pilot called his wingman: 'Hey Murph, I just want to let you know our plane's running a bit late here, and you might want to call the client.' He had no idea that two planes had crashed into the World Trade Center towers. Neither did the captain of the commercial jet. They sat there for another hour and a half, before finally returning to the gate and allowing the passengers out.

Bolting off the plane, Bourke called his home Air National Guard unit in Fresno, California. 'Get your tail here right now, Major Bourke!' said the commander. 'We're manning 24-hour combat patrols over San Francisco and Los Angeles, and you've got to get here!'

'Sir, I'm in Vermont. There's no way I can get there.' The commander didn't miss a beat: 'Well, go to the Vermont Air National Guard. They may need your help. You're activated.'

So, dressed as an average corporate type, Bourke took a taxi to the other side of the airport, and introduced himself to the security guard at the gate of the Vermont Air National Guard. The commanding officer came down to meet him. 'Son, are you the Afterburner guy that's stuck here?' 'Yes, sir, that's me.' The general leaned closer. 'You F-16 qualified?' 'Yes, sir.'

'What size boots do you wear? I am short one pilot,' said the general. 'We need twelve pilots to man 24-hour combat air patrols, and I'm short by one. You're on a flight in two hours.'

And that was that. Bourke walked into a briefing room just in time for the brief, listened to a 90-minute briefing, suited up, and was in the air. This California pilot was in a Vermont F-16 with guys he'd never met before, and flew with them for the next seven days.

How is that possible? Standards. Air force standards are so thorough, the training so strong, that Bourke could appear just in time for a briefing and fly for a week, no questions asked.

This commitment to standards is not as common in business as it is in the military, but that only makes it more powerful when it's used. It is a competitive advantage that can be used every day, whether your business is pizza or palaces. At McKinsey & Co, there are drilled standards on how teams approach problem solving, and how they communicate their answers. The results of those standards are anything but common; but it's the common approach that makes the difference. Anyone from any McKinsey office can walk into a room with other consultants they've not met before, with or without clients, and start work immediately, no questions asked. They are not getting paid to get to know each other, or how their team should work. That's what their training is for.

You can ask the same question of John Schnatter, the founder and CEO of Papa John's Pizza—still. You really have to listen to a guy who's created the world's most successful pizza business from scratch. John decided to go into pizzas when he was a dishwasher in his father's tavern, seeing the brutal evidence of what people liked and didn't like. 'Dad, people never return the pizza. The pizza's always gone. I noticed that people are particular about the crust. They don't touch it if it's soggy or too thick, but the pizza's always eaten.' So John literally knocked out the wall at the back of the broom closet in his father's kitchen, and started making pizza.

There are now 4700 Papa John restaurants in 33 countries. How much do they differ? Not at all. That's the secret. When Murph met John, he asked a question he often asks clients: 'Where's your pain?' The answer was stunning.

'My pain is that about 15 percent of our franchises are under-performing. They don't adhere to our standards. They want to sell chicken wings. They want to discount pizza. They want thicker-crust pizza. But we've told them how to make a perfect pizza. That's our business. We know what works. It's a simple business, Murph. We make pizzas. And if you make it the way we tell you to, you'll have a healthy franchise. We've got the statistical data. We've got the right system. We've got the right plan. We've got Pizza University, and put millions of dollars into perfect training. We've given our people every asset that they need, but 15 percent just don't get it. Just make the perfect pizza. Our mission in life, Murph, our only mission, is to make the perfect pizza.'[1]

So how do you get people to make the perfect pizza every time? That's what had John stumped for years. He set a scale for quality, and knew that a 7/10 pizza would make a franchise money, and a 6/10 pizza would lose. 'We hired the best training people in the world, and we put in training and software packages. And then we did this.' And he showed Murph a set of pictures. 'Here's a two and a half pizza. Here's a four and a half. That's a six and a half. That's an eight and a half. And that's a ten. Can you see a difference, Murph?' You bet he could.

Pizzas are near the universal food. You can buy a pizza in every suburb in the world, but no one will argue with Papa John's record. He's beaten them all. Voted best pizza in over 100 U.S. markets including Los Angeles, Washington DC, Dallas, Phoenix. Ranked number one by the American Customer Satisfaction Index for thirteen of the last fifteen years. How? With these standards, and these pictures. Keep it simple.

TRAINING: YOUR BEST AT THE READY

You can't run a Flex business without standards, and you can't have standards without training. In business, training has a bad name. In some countries, there's even been legislation to force businesses to do it! Senior executives do their darnedest to avoid it, and the whole exercise is organized to distract the business as little as possible from making money. The common view is 'we don't have time to train, because we're living and breathing our mission every day'.

Our answer? In the military, we were pretty busy too. We called it combat. We *trained during combat*. Why? Because wars aren't won on one mission. They are sustained campaigns, and we have to keep getting better throughout. As importantly, we have to keep our critical skills from getting rusty, because we never know when we'll need them, and when we do our lives and our mission might rely on them. It's a reason we like the more recent James Bond films. Daniel Craig is always working out, always fit, always ready for a 60-minute slugfest with an impossibly iron-framed villain. The workouts Roger Moore used to do looked fun, but lacked credibility for his mission. There's nothing worse than a Bond film without realism.

To what level do we train? We agree with the great sports coaches of our time, the likes of John Wooden, the 'Wizard of Westwood' who coached the UCLA basketball team to ten NCAA national championships in twelve years, including seven in a row. No other team has won two in a row. Wooden recognized that, 'The time to prepare isn't after you have been given the opportunity. It's long before the opportunity arises. Once the opportunity arrives, it's too late to prepare.'[2] For that reason, 'The pressure I created during practices may have exceeded that which opponents produced. I believe when an individual constantly works under pressure, he or she will respond automatically when faced with it during competition.'[3] The exact same approach to training has kept the New Zealand All Blacks at the top of world rugby for a century: few if any games match the intensity of their own sessions.

You need your training to be ahead of your game. You need to be able to exercise your skills in a potentially stressful situation, without thinking. In those situations, the whole point is to keep your mind free for the new, complex, and dynamic challenges that reality is serving up to you. That is what Flex is all about. You don't want to have to focus on the stuff you already know. You keep your knife sharp.

There's another reason for training to this level. If you want to change your system to the HD Destination you're aiming at, you have to be able to move faster than that system. As John Warden puts it in *Winning in FastTime*, 'You won't win in the 21st century by merely reacting to change, or making incremental improvements to maintain your current position. To win, you must decide what you want your tomorrow to be, and then make it happen faster than the rate of change in your competitive environment.'[4]

How to train

In the intensive initial training we received in the air force, there was no real distinction between the standards we had to memorize, and the standards we could look up: we had to memorize the lot. Not long after, much of that memory had been wiped, and we were like everyone else in the air force and everyone out there at work. Some things we would use every day and never forget; some things we had to look up. We needed prompts: checklists. The checklists we could pull down in a cockpit were shorthand for everything we had once known, and the confidence and surety we got from them when it mattered most was enormous. But they were reminders to us, triggering the mental memory we developed in training.

No surprise, but fighter pilots have a four-step process to develop that mental memory:

- Step 1: Desired learning objectives (DLOs)
- Step 2: Demo/do
- Step 3: Discipline
- Step 4: Continuation training

Desired learning objectives (DLOs)

We were never left in any doubt how we were going to spend our time in training. Murph's training officer would stand before him and say: 'Go study this, Murph. This is how you do the Cuban eight maneuver. I want you to read about it tonight. Tomorrow,

I'm coming to your squadron, and I'm going to brief you on how to do a Cuban eight. Then we're going to demo/do. Sleep well.'

The DLOs are objectives, just like mission objectives: clear, measurable, actionable, and aligned. We need to be able to answer whether we achieved our DLO, whether it was to do the Cuban eight, to lay out a pizza with the right ingredients within a certain time, to write a string of code, or to make a sales call.

Demo/do, repeated

Have you ever tried to learn fishing knots or a dance step from a book? Reading about something is one thing, seeing it done by a person who knows what they're doing is something else. That's why so many millennials go straight to YouTube to learn anything, and skip the reading part. But they don't get to fast-track their learning by repeating the demo/do. Murph's training officer would greet him next morning: 'Read the manual? Good. I understand what the manual says, and that's what you think it means, but here's why we wrote it that way. Let me *show* you the Cuban eight. I'm going to show you how to do it, and then I want you to do it. And we're going to repeat that over and over again. We're going to demo/do, demo/do, demo/do.' That's what we did for a year, on every maneuver. We kept going for two years, doing the same maneuvers hundreds of times each. And out popped a fighter pilot. It's like the golfer Lee Trevino hitting a hole-in-one and being commended on his good luck. 'Luck? I've practiced 25 years for that shot!'

How does that work in business? It requires patience. People like to be pointed to the manual and to learn their own way, and their managers don't want to be overbearing, and don't want to waste time. But both miss out. Whether it's a routine maintenance, a new piece of software, a sales call, an investment pitch or a difficult conversation: the extra time up front pays. There is time to highlight the danger points and the shades of difficulty that don't appear in the manual, to find out that each individual may do part of it well, and another part poorly. It's demo/do, and it's repeated, so there's instant feedback before bad habits set in.

Discipline and continuation

The third step in training is discipline, self-discipline. That's the discipline to carry out the process, to stick by your standards, to fall back on your training. Without discipline, your standards aren't all that valuable, because there's not a concrete expectation that they will be met. Discipline is what makes you be the person other people want to work with, because they can rely on you. Nobody is going to stand over you to *make* you keep your work habits and standards sharp, so it's up to you. Back in Chapter 5, 'The Flex team', we learned about the U.S. Army Rangers, and the Ranger Assessment and Selection Program (RASP) and, for those who make it through, Ranger School. We might not have the discipline and intensity of those Rangers, but they are the gold standard. Their training not only underpins their skills, but generates the mental toughness and courage needed for their missions.

This is also true for continuation training, which is mandatory for pilots and for professionals such as lawyers, doctors, and accountants. It keeps our thinking on new and old standards fresh. There's a strong argument for regular sessions on the critical standards to be used in more businesses. Often these are done through online courses, quick quizzes over a lunch break. But people clicking those multiple-choice boxes aren't engaged in what they're learning. They're not discussing it with their peers, testing whether the standards do or don't work. Using Flex, new standards will be taken up by teams through the execution cycle. Other teams won't have heard about these changes, or if they have won't have heard the stories of why they were needed. In our own firm, we spend two days a year, all together, working over our standards and how they've been refined. Being pilots that feels natural.

BUILDING AND TAPPING SITUATIONAL STANDARDS

We've talked a lot about learning and standards, and many may correctly imagine that in the military there are vast manuals covering every possible procedure. In areas where there are serious safety risks this is appropriate, and those industries know what they have to do to maintain their standards and safety. But for general business practices, the things that determine whether a business will be successful or not in getting things done, such manuals either don't exist or are not referred to.

Flex is an agile methodology that brings recent lessons learned into each mission. Yet there is still a need to capture and store those lessons learned for other teams in the business, lessons that are needed for particular situations every now and then, rather than the mandatory everyday procedures. These systems must be as simple as possible, both to capture lessons learned and to draw on them as needed.

Given the power of our modern IT tools, we think only four things are needed:

- a searchable, electronic file folder, and logical sub-folders, accessible to all who need it
- a standard file-naming protocol that makes it clear what's in the file (to help rank your searches for relevance)
- the discipline to put lessons learned into those folders after a debrief, and
- the expectation that you run a free search for what you need when you're planning a mission.

Little more, then, than is sitting on your desktop now.

15

KICKSTARTING FLEX

Flex won't just happen for you. You can adopt it yourself with little delay, and see what a difference it makes. For your teams to adopt Flex takes a little more effort. Like any change you ask of your teams, you'll need to convince people of its good sense, demonstrate it yourself, give people the support they need, and consider consequences good and bad. You'll need your teams to commit to their execution rhythm, and to sing Flex to that rhythm until those new habits take hold.

You might be surprised to hear us say that it really doesn't matter too much where you start with Flex. Of course it would be nice if you followed the script from top to bottom: got your team together, built High-definition (HD) Destination, set your strategies, fixed on your wings, put your teams in place to run their missions, and let the Flex execution engine fire up. But we know that's not going to happen.

Rather, start wherever you find yourself, today. If a mission is coming up, schedule a planning session for it, and then do your homework to prepare for that session. If you're on a mission that seems a little off track, do an X-Gap and find out exactly where you are so that you can reset the mission and its plan. If you've just completed a mission, take a moment to try a debrief, carefully and patiently at first, setting the right tone by volunteering what you as leader could have done differently. Set your expectations low at first, follow the advice in this book, and grab the opportunity to pre-plan the next mission.

Just get started. The whole point of Flex is to learn by doing, and get better every time.

RECAPPING FLEX

Flex is a way of thinking and a framework for action that helps you to do the right things, very well.

Flex thinking

The Flex way of thinking engages people by balancing direction and autonomy, speed and consideration, simplicity and dynamism, reliability and creativity, process and awareness.

The Flex framework for action is the ideal way to learn the Flex balances and apply them in action. The Flex engine of plan–brief–execute–debrief develops our thinking by matching the four ways in which adults learn best: consider, process, experience, review.

Flex framework for action

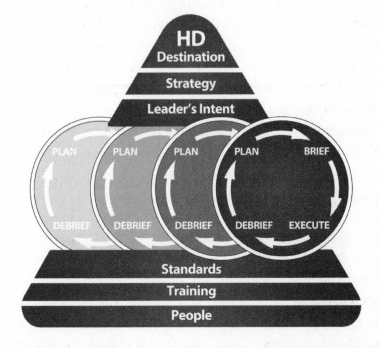

- **HD Destination.** The complete image of what all of your organization's missions are aiming for.
- **Strategy.** How your organization will get to its HD Destination.
- **Leader's intent.** How your mission leader intends the mission to support the strategy.
- **Plan.** The team deciding *who* does *what* by *when* to meet the leader's intent, and *why* and *what-if*.
- **Brief.** A direct, personal, and concise communication of the plan by the leader, that calls the team and each individual from thought to action.
- **Execute.** The team working through its planned course of action, without becoming task saturated, adjusting it as needed, with collective responsibility and individual accountability.
- **Debrief.** A blameless review of what happened, win or lose, and what can be learned from it.

- **Standards.** The part of every team and plan that everyone knows and everyone can rely on, whether or not it's said.
- **Training.** How to know and rely on your standards.
- **People.** All you've got. Take care of them.

Flex won't just happen for you. You can adopt it yourself with little delay, and see what a difference it makes. For your teams to adopt Flex takes a little more effort. Like any change you ask of your teams, you'll need to convince people of its good sense, demonstrate it yourself, give people the support they need, and consider consequences good and bad. You'll need your teams to commit to their execution rhythm, and to sing Flex to that rhythm until those new habits take hold.

Flex teams

Flex teams should be made up of around five to twelve people who share a common mission: big enough to have the skills and diversity the mission needs, and small enough for each team member to know and rely on and to care for each other.

Flex planning

The more complex a plan, the more likely it will fail. Flex planning is fast, yet considered—so that you have an effective plan when you need it. The resulting plan is simple, yet dynamic—so that it nails the objective, changing as it needs to. And the plan is direct, yet empowering—so that people have clear accountability, and keep the initiative they need. A Flex plan calls on your team to be engaged on their mission, not robotic as follows:

- **Open planning.** Get the team leaders responsible for executing the mission in the room. Don't make and deliver a plan for others to execute.

- **Leader's intent.** The mission's intended effect, at which the objective is targeted.
- **Objective.** Clear, measurable, achievable. Set by the team, not by the leader. Will likely evolve through the planning process.
- **Threats.** Internal or external? If controllable, that control becomes part of the plan. If not, park it as a contingency. There is no 'risk management plan'.
- **Resources.** Every threat needs to be matched by a resource. Who and what, inside and outside your team.
- **Lessons learned.** Quick search of your memories and database for things to do or not do in this situation.
- **Course of action.** Who (the individual), does what by when. As simple as that.
- **Red Team.** Test the course of action by people who've been there before.
- **Contingencies.** For the most likely uncontrollable threats, what is your trigger for action, and the action you'll take?

Briefing

The plan is only finalized in the acts of writing it up and delivering it as the brief. The brief is the cut-off: time to stop doubt, stop uncertainty, stop planning, and start executing. Brief the plan and fly the brief.

The brief is the *only* one-way communication in all of Flex. It is the leader's time to take accountability for the mission, to set his or her style, and to reinforce the expected team culture and standards. Be early. Be meticulous. Put the briefing steps up on the wall behind the team:

- **B**ig picture (HD Destination, situation, intent)
- **R**estate (mission objective)
- **I**dentify (threats and resources)

- **E**xecute (your course of action)
- **F**lexibility (the contingencies)

No surprises. Check for understanding. Are people looking at you, are they distracted? If so, use 'pose, pause, pounce' to switch everyone back on. Finish with a positive call to launch the mission.

Keeping people to the plan

People are human and don't always stick to the plan. Take steps to guard against the risks of inattention or task saturation. Errors track saturation like ants track honey. Look out for people shutting down, doing lots of little things without doing the big things, spending too long getting stuff 'organized' before getting the important stuff done, blocking out what's important around them. Use the tools that keep people to their plan:

- **A dashboard with primary and cross-check indicators.** Each team and mission has its own primary indicator. Only the CEO has the firm's profitability.
- **Your wingman (mutual support).** Your second eyes and ears.
- **Clear, concise communication.** Standards that you all use to keep every interaction sharp and understood.
- **Task shedding.** What *must* you do? *Should* do? *Nice to* do? *Do last*, if at all?
- **Checklists.** There are two critical rules for a checklist: keep it simple, and use it. The people doing the actions create the checklists: one page, trigger points, nine steps or less. Using checklists calms nerves and eliminates errors. If possible, two people check off 'Do–Confirm'. Keep emergency and reference checklists where they can be found fast.

Keeping the plan to reality

Plans have to adapt because the reality of a situation changes. Every plan includes team check-in points to X-Gap: to analyze and 'cross the gap' between the plan and its execution. Each X-Gap is a decision point for the mission: continue, adjust, or abort? Green light, yellow, or red? Depending on your mission, set them hourly, daily or weekly as a regular event: the markers of your execution rhythm. An X-Gap is not a meeting. Allow for no more than two minutes at the top, two minutes per task review, and two minutes at the end. Use B-R-I-E-F, again.

Debrief

A STEALTH debrief is your secret weapon, both for learning and for a positive working culture. It gives closure to the mission, bottles momentum for larger efforts, and builds leadership. Debrief immediately after every mission—win, lose or draw—as an integral part of the mission itself using the following technique:

- **Set up.** Prepare the time, the place, the people, the materials, yourself.
- **Tone.** Nameless, rankless, starting with the leader's own mistakes.
- **Execution against objective.** Flex objectives are measurable. Did you meet them?
- **Analysis of execution.** How and why did we succeed or fail?
- **Lessons learned.** What clear lessons did we learn from this mission?
- **Transfer of lessons.** Who needs this lesson, how fast, and how will we get it to them?
- **High note.** End the debrief, and the mission, with a positive sense of accomplishment.

Situational awareness

If your team doesn't know what its threats are, or doesn't know the effects of its actions, it's just 'tumbleweed'. Using the Flex cycle builds two types of situational awareness (or 'SA'). It keep line-of-sight alignment from your actions, through your mission objective, to your organizational HD Destination. It appreciates that you are always working within a system, and anything you do will have an effect on that system. Teams build these awareness skills just as they build their execution skills.

Flex in organizations

Flex is *designed* to be scalable: to be used independently or in unison by multiple teams at any level of an organization. Flex can be used to set an organizational objective and course of action, in just the same way as for a smaller mission plan. The difference is that there are more than one facets to an organizational objective—the HD Destination—and that some missions will have to make or break the organization's systems. Before committing your resources, test that your organizational objective and strategy meet the Flex tests.

Standards and training

Organizational and personal standards make personal initiative and creativity possible. These are the wings that, as a company and individually, you want to rely on without thinking. Keep lessons and standards at your fingertips, filed and easily searched by modern personal computers and smartphones. You can't run a Flex business without standards, and you can't have standards without training. Learn your standards and skills with demo/do, repeated as often as needed, then the discipline to keep them sharp. Discipline is what makes you be the person other people want to work with, because they can rely on you.

RECAPPING WHAT YOU'RE AIMING FOR

In this book, we've done our best to share with you the principles that were designed to get things done by novice fighter pilots flying state-of-the-art jets. They are now being used well beyond fighter squadrons and elite military units. Flex helps you build great teams, great firms, and to create great leaders and followers.

Great followers and leaders

In the elite wings of the U.S. and Australian military, young men and women have been given the responsibility of leading missions, squadrons, and units, and given wings at a very young age, and in most cases without any prior experience. They are entrusted to take people and equipment, highly valued in every sense of the word, into hostile and complex environments, to fulfill their mission there, and to get them home safe. With incredibly high reliability, they do so.

It's clichéd to say that great leaders start off as great followers, but they do. By the time these young men and women lead their own missions, they will have been on any number of missions and served under leaders who are as diverse in character and style as they are. Yet the similarities are clear and comforting: following Flex principles apply equally to leaders and to followers, and of course you need both to dance well:

- Respectful truth over artificial harmony.
- Knowing when to make the decisions that mark leadership, and when to be a nameless, rankless team member.
- Knowing their team members and making their welfare paramount.
- Knowing how to ensure a mission serves an aligned purpose.
- Insisting on standard operating procedures, including brief, clear communication.

- Ensuring team members know what to do, but are not told how to do it.
- Respecting the power of the Flex framework for action and a way of thinking.

Great teams

Whether your organization is seven- or 7 million-people strong, whether its structure is flat or hierarchical, its work is usually done by teams of around seven people, the golden number favored in organizational research. They may be self-forming or designated from on high, and their work may be self-driven or delegated to them as part of a greater effort, but a team of five to ten people will come together to get the job done. If these teams don't work well, it is very much harder to reach the firm's objectives, or for individuals in the firm to grow professionally. We need our teams to work.

Flex helps build great teams by:

- Giving them a common language and a shared mental model for thought and action.
- Ensuring team members have the diverse skills and experience needed for the job.
- Engaging all members of the team in planning, executing, and debriefing their work.
- Tapping into experts with greater experience and situational awareness.
- Ensuring that their missions are what the organization needs.
- Making members individually accountable for their part of the mission.
- Giving them clear decision-making authority and the means to exercize it.
- Giving them the support they need to stay focussed and effective.

- Ensuring that they draw on and contribute to situational awareness and standards that they and other teams rely on.
- Giving them great followers and leaders.

Great firms

A firm that succeeds in a single year's priorities or a three-year strategy has done well. Yet the turnover of firms in the Fortune 500 and other topline lists demonstrates how hard it is to do so year after year, strategy after strategy. For success, a firm needs not only to be able to get things done, but for it to build the capability to do so consistently, following a coherent strategy towards an inspiring vision, both of which keep pace with industry and social change.

Flex's framework for action helps deliver these with:

- HD Destinations that complement a corporate vision or purpose, but are more detailed and actionable.
- Situational awareness of the networks and systems on the path to an HD Destination.
- Missions that have clear line of sight to the HD Destinations, either as part of a strategy to change a system, or to perform more effectively within a system.
- Performance engines, accountability, and culture to deliver those missions.
- Debriefing that pivots your organization ahead of your industry's rate of change and complexity.
- Continual refreshing of situational awareness and standards to do so reliably.
- Great teams to get all these jobs done.

You've been briefed. Flex is as close as you want it to be.

OUR PILOTS
(ACKNOWLEDGEMENTS)

In particular, we would like to thank our fellow pilots who have flown with us in the air force, at Afterburner, and in writing this book: Aaron 'Tuck' Tucker, Aaron 'Wardy' Ward, Amy 'Sable' Lewis, Charles 'Chaz' Campbell, Chris Gomez, Christiaan 'Serge' Durrant, David 'Finch' Guenthner, Jake Duffy, Joe 'Gusto' Connolly, Joel 'Thor' Neeb, Patrick 'Lips' Houlahan, Phil Eldridge, Scott 'Gunner' Leonard, Simon 'Slash' Ashworth, Steve 'Zed' Roberton, Tom 'Mad Dog' Friend, and Tracey 'JackieO' LaTourette.*

As with any mission, this book needed more than just pilots. Thanks to Will Duke, who has captured and guided our intellectual property as Afterburner's Director of Learning and Development since our inception. Thanks to Crystal Tarasin and Cat Stirn at Afterburner who have supported our efforts to the hilt. Thanks to the wonderful editors and designers at Allen & Unwin: Elizabeth Weiss, Christa Munns, Julia Cain, Michelle Swainson and Simon Rattray. And thank you to Josh Dowse, consultant, eco-warrior and ghost writer who worked tirelessly to pull together a diverse bunch of fighter pilots from different countries, clients and managing the entire publishing process on our behalf. A true Flex practitioner.

* Fighter pilot call signs are, for the most part, chosen by peers to be hard to live with.

NOTES

1. The origins of Flex

1   The G-force is the pressure a pilot feels when the plane is changing either its speed or its direction, up or down or side to side—just what a driver feels in a car going too fast around a corner.

2   Australian Defence Force, *Joint Military Appreciation Process*, ADFP 5.0.1, Introduction.

3   Today, Afterburner works with armed forces on veteran transition, using Flex to guide veterans through that very question: 'Now what?'

2. What is Flex?

1   Quoted in Damon Hack, 'One Giant Leap for Manningkind', *Sports Illustrated*, 13 February 2012.

2   Mark Tedrow, US Navy Blue Angels, 'Blue Angels', YouTube http://www.allreadable.com/d59f6wo9.

3. The Flex framework for action

1   Tracy 'JackieO' LaTourette, interview 21 March 2016.

4. The Flex way of thinking

1   PwC 2015, *Millennials at Work: Reshaping the workplace*.

2   The skill–will matrix is a common management tool, but this version from Dan Spira (danspira.com) captures it well. Dan Spira ©2010.

3   Edgar H. Schein, in foreword to Amy C. Edmondson, *Teaming: How*

organizations, learn, innovate, and compete in the knowledge economy, Jossey-Bass, New York, 2012.

4   D. Kahneman, *Thinking, Fast and Slow,* Farrar, Straus and Giroux, New York, 2011.

5   James Surowiecki, *The Wisdom of Crowds,* Anchor, New York, 2005.

6   Adapted from Scott E. Page, *The Difference: How the power of diversity creates better groups, firms, schools, and society,* Princeton University Press, 2007, p. 361.

7   Dan Lovallo and Olivier Sibony, 'The case for behavioral strategy', *McKinsey Quarterly,* March 2010.

8   Jim Collins and Morten Hansen, *Great by Choice,* HarperBusiness, New York, 2011, p. 21.

9   Collins and Hansen, *Great by Choice,* p. 21.

10 Rita McGrath, 'The pace of technology adoption is speeding up.' *Harvard Business Review,* November 2013.

11 Anne Mulcahy, 'How we do it: Three executives reflect on strategic decision making', *McKinsey Quarterly,* March 2010.

12 John A. Warden III and Leland A. Russell, *Winning in Fast Time,* GEO Group Press, Newport Beach, 2001.

5. The Flex team

1   Future Workplace (2012), 'Multiple generations at work'. http://futureworkplace.com/wp-content/uploads/MultipleGenAtWork_infographic.pdf. Accessed 13 May 2016.

6. Flex planning

1   E.L. Deci, J.P. Connell and R.M. Ryan, 'Self-determination in a work organization', *Journal of Applied Psychology,* 1989, 74, pp. 580–90. Quoted in Gagne and Deci, 'Self-determination theory and work motivation', *Journal of Organizational Behavior,* 2005, 26, pp. 331–62.

2   PwC 2015, *Millennials at Work: Reshaping the workplace.*

3   Donald Sull, *The Upside of Turbulence,* HarperBusiness, New York, 2009.

4   Originally published in the March 1899 issue of the magazine *Philistine* by its editor, Elbert Hubbart, and then turned by him into a pamphlet and a book: https://en.wikipedia.org/wiki/A_Message_to_Garcia. Accessed 24 November 2015.

5   Charles Duhigg, *The Power of Habit,* Random House, New York, 2012.

7. The six-step mission planning process

1   Walt Kelly was nodding to a line from 140 years earlier. After the fledgling U.S. Navy defeated and captured six British vessels in the 1813 Battle

of Lake Erie, Commodore Oliver Hazard Perry reported back: 'We have met the enemy and they are ours. Two ships, two brigs, one schooner and one sloop.'

2 Jim Collins and Morten Hansen, *Great by Choice*, HarperBusiness, New York, 2011.

3 D. Hofstadter: *Gödel, Escher, Bach: An eternal golden braid*. 20th anniversary edn, 1999, p. 152.

4 D. Kahneman, *Thinking, Fast and Slow*, Farrar, Straus and Giroux, New York, 2011.

8. Brief (putting your plan into action)

1 Interview, Professor Donald Sull, 9 December 2015.

9. Execute (keeping people to the plan)

1 U.S. Coast Guard Research & Development Center, Report CG-10-21-00 *Communications Problems in Marine Casualties*, October 2000.

2 Example from Afterburner colleague 'Dingee'.

3 Atul Gawande, *The Checklist Manifesto: How to get things right*, Picador, London, 2011.

10. X-Gaps and execution rhythm

1 Usually paraphrased as 'When the facts change, I change my mind. What do you do, sir?': https://en.wikiquote.org/wiki/John_Maynard_Keynes#The_General_Theory_of_Employment.2C_Interest_and_Money_.281936.29. Accessed 24 November 2015.

2 Dan Ariely, *Predictably Irrational: The hidden forces that shape our decisions*, Harper, New York, 2008.

11. The debrief

1 A. Kinkhabwala, 'The New York Giants take to practicing military precision', *The Wall Street Journal*, 9 November 2011.

2 Scott Tannenbaum and Christopher P. Cerasoli, 'Do team and individual debriefs enhance performance? A meta-analysis', *Human Factors*, February 2013, 55(1), pp. 231–45.

3 Noel Tichy and Warren Bennis, *Judgment*, Portfolio, New York, 2009.

4 Interview, Patrick 'Lips' Houlahan, 11 December 2015.

5 Interview, Patrick 'Lips' Houlahan.

6 Jim Collins and Morten Hansen, *Great by Choice*, HarperBusiness, New York, 2011.

7 Peter M. Senge, *The Fifth Discipline: The art and practice of the learning organization*, Doubleday, New York, 2006, p. 226.

8 John P. Kotter, *XLR8: Building strategic ability for a faster-moving world*, HBR Press, Boston, 2014.

9 J.P. Shapiro, 'America's best hospitals', *US News and World Report*, 17 July 2000.
10 Jim Collins, *Good to Great*, HarperBusiness, New York, 2001.
11 Jim Collins, *How the Mighty Fall*, Jim Collins Publishing, 2009.

12. Situational awareness
1 Greg Satell, 'A look back at why Blockbuster really failed and why it didn't have to', *Forbes*, 5 September 2014.
2 Anita M. Rothblum, 'Human factors in incident investigation and analysis', US Coast Guard R&D Center, April 2002.

13. Flex in organizations
1 https://m.facebook.com/amazon/info. Accessed 24 November 2015.
2 Dan McAtee, interview, 11 August 2013.
3 John P. Kotter, *A Sense of Urgency*, Harvard Business School Press, 2008.
4 Martin Luther King, 'I have a dream', Lincoln Memorial, Washington D.C. 28 August 1963.
5 Coca-Cola company, 'Mission, Vision & Values', http://www.coca-colacompany.com/our-company/mission-vision-values/. Accessed 24 November 2015.
6 John A. Warden III and Leland A. Russell, *Winning in FastTime*, Venturist Publishing, Alabama, 2002.
7 Gusto served in the U.S. Army for seven years where he was Airborne and Ranger qualified. In his final assignment he served as a company commander, and has since worked in a range of senior executive positions in both aggressive private equity and more conservative commercial banking companies. He has applied and developed the Flex-like principles he learned as a Ranger throughout that career, and is now a senior client adviser with Afterburner.
8 Michael Porter, *Competitive Strategy*, The Free Press, New York, 1980, p. 17.
9 Scott Batjos, interview, 21 March 2016.

14. The Flex wings
1 John Schnatter, interview, 2004.
2 John Wooden, *Wooden: A lifetime of observations and reflections on and off the court*, McGraw-Hill, New York, 1997, p. 130.
3 John Wooden, ibid., p. 135.
4 John A. Warden III and Leland A. Russell, *Winning in FastTime*, Venturist Publishing, Alabama, 2002.

INDEX